SOMERVILLE THE SOLDIER

Somerville
the Soldier

A PLAY BY

DONALD CAMPBELL

PAUL HARRIS PUBLISHING

EDINBURGH

822
CAM

First published
by PAUL HARRIS PUBLISHING
25 London Street, Edinburgh
1976

© *Copyright Donald Campbell 1978*

British Library Cataloguing in Publication Data
    Campbell, Donald, b.1940
        Somerville the Soldier.
        I. Title
        822'.9'14   PR6053.A482S/
        ISBN 0-904505-54-5

Published with the financial assistance of the Scottish Arts Council

Printed in Scotland
by THE SHETLAND TIMES LTD
Lerwick, Shetland

INTRODUCTION

'All reform except a moral one' wrote Thomas Carlyle in his *Corn Law Rhymes* 'will prove unavailing'. That thought was very much in my mind when I wrote this play. By a strange coincidence, at almost the precise moment that Carlyle arrived in London to begin his glittering literary career, the city received another visitor with whom Carlyle had much in common but who, at that moment in time, had been accorded a fame that was infinitely greater than any that even the Sage of Chelsea would later enjoy. This visitor was Alexander Somerville, usually referred to as 'the Scots Grey' or 'Somerville the Soldier'.

Like Carlyle, Somerville came from Lowland Scottish peasant stock and had been brought up under the rigorous disciplines of Scottish Presbyterianism. Unlike Carlyle, he had not been given the opportunity to attend a University, nor could he be said to have an intellect that was anything as bright as that of his brilliant contemporary. For all that, Somerville was by no means unlettered: even before his short-lived career as a private in the Scots Greys, he had written poems and newspaper articles. His most famous piece of writing, however, was a letter he had written to the *Birmingham Weekly Dispatch* in the early summer of 1832.

It was a time of constitutional and political crisis. In the later stages of the Movement for Parliamentary Reform, there was a real danger of a military dictatorship (under the Duke of Wellington) taking over the government of Great Britain. As the radical Political Unions were preparing to march to London to agitate for the passing of the Reform Bill, the army was preparing to stop them. In Birmingham, where Somerville was stationed with the Scots Greys, the soldiers were confined to barracks, denied visitors and told to rough-grind their swords — an order usually associated with the containment of a civilian mob. Since the ordinary troopers supported Reform to a man, they were all appalled by this action — but it was Somerville who made the protest. In his letter to the paper, he declared that the Scots Greys 'would be the last to degrade themselves

5

below the dignity of British soldiers, in acting as the tools of the tyrant' and warned the Duke of Wellington that 'military government shall never again be set up in this country'.

Needless to say, the authorities were incensed. Major Wyndham, Somerville's C.O., lost no time in trumping up a charge against him, instituting a court-martial and sentencing Somerville to two hundred strokes of the cat-o-nine-tails. Somerville bore this dreadful punishment with so much fortitude that, after only half the punishment had been carried out, Wyndham felt forced to call a halt and have Somerville cut down. No doubt, the C.O. was afraid that Somerville might die and cause even more trouble.

The matter did not rest there, however. Somehow or other (most probably through Somerville's press contacts) the story got out, questions were asked in the now-Reformed House of Commons and Somerville was granted a Court of Enquiry. As a result of this, he was pardoned, given an honourable discharge and paid the sum of £250 in compensation. On leaving the service, he went to London where he tried, for a time, to lead the life of an ordinary private citizen. This was to prove impossible: he had caught the imagination of the masses and wherever he went he was treated to adulation and acclaim. Being modest and retiring by nature, Somerville was unable to stomach this and returned to Scotland where, among other things, he tried to found a literary magazine in Edinburgh — a venture which proved both unsuccessful and disillusioning. Somerville had no choice but to go back to London, where William Cobbett had promised to help him gain a foothold in journalism. It is at this point that my play begins.

DONALD CAMPBELL
Edinburgh, June 1978

DEDICATION

This play is dedicated
to
Gavin Douglas Campbell

SOMERVILLE THE SOLDIER *was first performed at the Traverse Theatre, Edinburgh, on June 1 1978, with the following cast:*

KATE BARBOUR	*B E T H R O B E N S*
CHARLEY TYLER	*J I M M Y Y U I L L*
SALLY, Kate's daughter	*M A R I A N B O Y E S*
HARRY HAMPDEN, Kate's brother	*R O L A N D O L I V E R*
CAPTAIN GILLIES	*R O Y H A N L O N*
DUNCAN CRAIG	*F I N L A Y W E L S H*
ALEXANDER SOMERVILLE	*B E N N Y Y O U N G*

Directed by S A N D Y   N E I L S O N
Presented by T H E   T R A V E R S E   T H E A T R E
Stage Manager S A N D R A   D A V I D S O N
Designer T A N Y A   M c C A L L I N
Lighting designed by A L A S T A I R   M c A R T H U R

8

SOMERVILLE DRAGOON

Oh Sandy Simmerill is my name
From Springfield in the Lammermoors I came
And many's the time I've cursed the day
I took the shilling and signed my life away

Chorus
For I am a trooper bold
Sworn to do as I am told
But you cannot buy my soul
With your thirteen pence a day

I've hedged and ditched, I've ploughed and reaped
I've quarried out stone and I've shorn the sheep
Till I tired of living on oats and whey
To Birmingham I came as a trooper in the Greys

In thirty two the trouble came
Two hundred thousand working men
To Newhall Hill bold Attwood drew
Who swore they'd march to force the Reform Bill through

In the barracks then we troopers found
Our cutlasses must be rough-ground
Our officers soon let us know
The Chartist mob it was to be our foe

To the *Weekly Dispatch* I then did write
To make it known as best I might
No oath I took can make me fight
With honest men who seek their peaceful rights

Then on Monday twenty-eighth of May
In the riding school was made great play
My horse they goaded till I was tossed
Then for court martial straight they did me post

9

The Major Windham sneered at me
"We'll teach you how to write" said he
"We'll see your backbone, never fear
Two hundred strokes of the cat will be your share"

The stripped me of my stock and coat
They staked me out like a dumb scape-goat
The hospital sergeant stood nearby
Then Farrier Simpson swung the cat on high

Well he did his duty and he laid it on
My back he flayed, and the blood did run
One hundred I took without a cry
Then they cut me down for fear that I should die

For I am a trooper bold
Sworn to do as I am told
But you cannot buy my soul
With your thirteen pence a day

Ian Campbell

CHARACTERS

KATE BARBOUR

CHARLEY TYLER

SALLY, Kate's daughter

HARRY HAMPDEN, Kate's brother

CAPTAIN GILLIES

DUNCAN CRAIG

ALEXANDER SOMERVILLE

The action takes place in the sitting-room of the flat above Harry Hampden's pub, somewhere in London, during the week 15th - 21st April 1834. The room may be described as follows: in the foreground there are two rather bulky armchairs; behind them is a table with four chairs; to the right of the table, against the back wall, there is a dresser; on the wall to the left of the dresser, hangs a picture of a man in military uniform. There are a number of books, papers, pen and ink and a box of matches on the dresser. There are two entrances, the left coming in from the rest of the house, the right coming in from Somerville's bedroom.

LANGUAGE

In general, I have used standard forms — both Scots and English — leaving the idioms and speech-rhythms of the dialogue to be overlaid by regional accents. In Somerville's case, however, I have introduced a degree of dialect spelling and it is *very important* that this should be maintained in performance.

SONG AND POEM

My thanks are due to Ian Campbell for allowing me to use his song, *Somerville, Dragoon* in both the performance and publication of this play, as well as quoting it within the body of the text. Since I have been unable to trace any of Somerville's own poems, I have taken the liberty of composing *My love, I see you as a light* on his behalf.

11

ACT ONE

SCENE ONE

Monday evening. Enter KATE BARBOUR, *carrying a large tray of wine and glasses, followed by* CHARLEY TYLER. *Middle-aged, but still an attractive woman,* KATE *is a 'manager' of great vigour and intensity.* CHARLEY *is a young man in his early twenties, wearing what is obviously his best suit. Youthful gaucherie combines with natural aggressiveness to give him a pugnacious, often surly, manner.* KATE *sets the tray down on the table and calls in the direction of the right-hand door.*

KATE *(calling)* Sally! Sall-ee! you there, girl?

SALLY *(off)* Yes, Mum! Coming!

KATE *(calling)* What you doing? *(Turns and indicates the left-hand chair to* CHARLEY.*)* Sit down, Charley!

SALLY *(off)* Just getting the Soldier's room straight, that's all!

KATE *(calling)* Best get a move on, then! They won't be long now!

SALLY *(off)* Nearly finished!

Responding to KATE'S *command,* CHARLEY *takes a seat.* KATE *goes to the right-hand chair and sits down wearily.*

KATE *(with a sigh)* Oh! Thank God to get off my feet!

CHARLEY Had a busy day, then, Mrs B?

KATE Busy? Huh, you don't know the half of it, Charley Tyler! If I was to tell you all I've done today — well, you'd never believe me, that's all!

Enter SALLY, *a pretty girl in her late teens. She grins to* CHARLEY *and takes a seat at the table.*

SALLY Wotcher, Charley!

CHARLIE *(nods)* Sal!

SALLY What you doing here, then?

KATE Been elected to the committee, ain't he?

SALLY Never! Well, good for you, Charley! *(To* KATE.*)* But, here — you ain't got a meeting tonight, have you?

KATE No! Well, not a meeting exactly — more of what you might call a delegation. *(Smiles to them both.)* To welcome the Soldier to London!

SALLY Oh, the Soldier! Just fancy — the Soldier, living in our house! *(Shakes her head.)* I still can't believe it, you know!

KATE Well, you better start believing it girl! Duncan Craig's gone off to fetch him now — and they shouldn't be long.

SALLY *(dreamily)* Somerville the Soldier! In our house! *(Pauses.)* Here, I wonder what he'll be like? To look at, I mean. What you reckon, Mum?

KATE Oh, I don't know! I ain't never seen him, have I?

CHARLEY I have.

SALLY Oh, Charley! Have you really? What was he like? Handsome, you reckon?

CHARLEY Handsome? I don't know about handsome. Ordinary sort of bloke, really. Tell you the truth, if I hadn't of known he was the Soldier, I'd never have guessed.

SALLY How's that, Charley?

CHARLEY Well, he ain't much to look at, you know, Sal! About my age, a bit taller than me, thinner. He was wearing a perfectly ordinary suit of clothes, smoking a pipe. Ask me, he looked just like any other working bloke!

KATE Where'd you see him, Charley?

CHARLEY Oh, it was a couple of years back, Mrs B. Just before they passed the Reform Bill. Me and some of the lads went down the Political Union — you know, Theobald's Road?

KATE Oh yes?

CHARLEY Old John Lawless had come over from Ireland and we thought we'd go and give him a listen. Fair old speaker,

14

John Lawless! Anyway, first I saw of the Soldier, he was sitting next to me Uncle Stan.

SALLY Get away!

CHARLEY Straight up, Sal! Of course, I didn't know he was the Soldier then, did I? But someone else must have done because all of a sudden like we hear this shout 'There he is! It's Somerville! Somerville the Soldier!' *(Laughs.)* And, before we all knew where we was, we was all up on our feet, clapping our hands, stamping the floor and cheering our bleeding heads off! *(Shakes his head.)* Oh, that was some night, I can tell you!

KATE And the Soldier? What did he do? Did he make a speech?

CHARLEY No. No, that was the funny thing. Most peculiar, that was!

SALLY How's that, Charley?

CHARLEY Well, we all *thought* he was going to speak, you know? He gets up and he goes off round the back — everybody thought he was going round to get up the platform. But no! He left the hall, the meeting, everything! Seems he didn't want to know!

KATE Well, that was funny!

CHARLEY Yes, I thought so and all — but me Uncle Stan, he reckoned that the Soldier had had just about as much as he could stand of that sort of thing.

SALLY What sort of thing?

CHARLEY Well, you know, Sal! Three cheers for Somerville and everything! All that fuss!

SALLY Well, what's the matter with that, then?

CHARLEY Me Uncle Stan reckons the Soldier's a modest sort of bloke what don't care for people fussing over him.

KATE You best watch that, Sally, while he's here.

SALLY Watch what, Mum?

KATE Don't go fussing over him. He don't like it.

SALLY *(sniffs)* I shall treat him the same as I treat any other guest! *(Pauses.)* How long's he staying, anyway?

KATE   Don't know. Until after the Revolution anyway, I should think. I expect you can count on that, at least!

SALLY *(sniggering)*   Hark at her, Charley! After the Revolution!

KATE   Well, we've got to face up to it, Sally! This country's been Revolution-ripe for the past two years! We've talked and planned and argued so much that we've got so that we can't hardly believe that this Revolution's ever going to come! Well, I've got news for you, Sally — the Revolution's coming all right! *(Winks to* CHARLEY.) It'll be here sooner than any of us think! Ain't I right, Charley?

CHARLEY   That's right, Mrs B. The time's coming when we'll have to stop talking about how to make the Revolution — and start talking about how to make it work!

Enter HARRY HAMPDEN. *Somewhat older than* KATE, *he is a voluble little man, easily excited, with a ferret-like temper and a manner that is deliberately coarse.*

KATE   Talking about getting things to work — here comes your Uncle Harry! I've been trying to get him to work for years!

SALLY *(Reprovingly)*   Oh, Mum!

HARRY *is carrying a newspaper and he taps* CHARLEY *on the shoulder with it.*

HARRY   All right, sonny-boy! Let's have you — move!

KATE   Harry!

CHARLEY *gets to his feet and moves over to sit beside* SALLY *at the table. He gestures to* KATE *that he doesn't mind doing this.*

CHARLEY   It's all right, Mrs B. Really it is! I'd rather sit here anyway.

HARRY *(to* KATE)   See? Good boy, that — knows his place. Knows who's master of this house, no mistake!

HARRY *sits down on his chair.*

16

KATE   It would be very nice, Harry Hampden, if, just once in a while, you made an effort to act civilised to my guests.

HARRY   Your guests? *Your* guests? Well, that's nice, I must say! That's very, very nice! *(Leans forward in his chair.)* Who's house is this, then? Eh? Who's fucking house is this? I spent twenty fucking years . . .

KATE   We'll have less of that, if you don't mind.

HARRY   Less of what? What you talking about?

KATE   You know what I mean, Harry Hampden! You want to think shame on yourself, you do! Young girl like Sally sitting here . . .

HARRY   *(Puzzled)*   Sally? What are you on about?

KATE   You know what I'm on about. What you said just now . . .

HARRY   Said? What'd I say?

SALLY   Forget it, Uncle Harry! Mum, please . . .

HARRY   No, I won't forget it! I want to know what I said to upset her ladyship here! Come on, Katie — tell me! What'd I say, eh? What'd I fucking say?

KATE   *(angrily)*   He said it again!

HARRY   Said what?

KATE   *(furiously)*   Fucking! You fucking said fucking!

HARRY   Oh, that's nice! Charming, that is. Charming language for a lady! Here, Charley — I'll bet your old mum don't use words like that!

By this time KATE *is on her feet, ready to physically attack* HARRY.

KATE   Harry Hampden, I swear I'll . . .

SALLY *rises and intervenes.*

SALLY   Mum! Uncle Harry! Please! Not tonight! Please don't let's have any rows tonight.

KATE *calms down.*

17

B

KATE Yes, Sally. You're quite right, of course. Best not encourage the old buzzard — tonight of all nights.

HARRY And what's so special about tonight, then? Eh? What's on the agenda tonight? Treason again, I expect. Treason against my King and country what I spent twenty fucking years . . .

KATE *(nearly screaming)* Oh, Harry, belt up for God's sake!

SALLY Yes, Uncle Harry, please! We got an important guest coming tonight, you see, and . . .

HARRY Important guest? Huh? Who's so bleeding important he comes to this house? Fergus O'Connor?

KATE You better tell him, Sally.

SALLY Alexander Somerville.

HARRY'S *jaw drops in astonishment.*

HARRY What? Not — not the soldier?

SALLY That's right, Uncle Harry. Somerville the Soldier.

HARRY Oh, My God! In this house — Somerville the Soldier's coming to my house?

KATE That's right, Harry. He's going to stop awhile and all.

HARRY Stop awhile? *(Almost beside himself, he leaps to his feet and bursts into song.)*

> "I am a trooper bold
> sworn to do as I am told
> but you cannot buy my soul
> with your thirteen pence a day! "

Ho, ho, this is a turnup for the book, eh? Somerville the Soldier, sleeping in this house!

KATE *(to* SALLY*)* I knew he'd be pleased!

A thought strikes HARRY.

HARRY Here — where's he going to sleep then?

KATE In the Captain's room.

HARRY *(delighted)* The Captain going to piss off then?

KATE *(with restraint)* The Captain is giving up his room for Mr Somerville in the meantime, yes!

HARRY Well, that's good news I must say! If there's one thing I hates more than officers what pretend to be gentlemen it's gentlemen what pretend to be officers!

KATE Harry, don't you dare start that again!

HARRY All right! All right! I know you fancy him! *(He pauses for* KATE *to rise to the jibe, but she refuses to be drawn.* HARRY *gives an anticipatory sigh.)* Somerville the Soldier, eh? *(Has a thought.)* Here — I wonder if it's true about the rum?

CHARLEY Rum?

HARRY Yes. You know. Don't you know the story about the rum? *(They all look blank, so he resumes his seat and relates it to them.)* Seems that just before they give him his punishment, one of his mates tried to slip him a bottle of rum, see? Fellow called Charley Hunter. 'No!' says the Soldier 'you hang on to that rum, Charley! I don't want none of it — not even a mouthful! They can cut me to pieces if they like, but I'm going to be sober while they're doing it! So just take away that there rum!' How about that then, eh?

CHARLEY Yes, he's a brave man all right!

KATE *(sighs)* The bravest of the brave!

HARRY Mind you — I have to say it — he's a right mug and all!

KATE Oh Harry!

SALLY How'd you make that out, Uncle Harry?

HARRY Well, it stands to reason, don't it? I mean, for starters he's a jock and . . .

KATE What the hell's the matter with that?

HARRY You want to let me finish, girl. I never said there was anything wrong with jocks, did I? I mean, apart from that drunken Scotch git that was daft enough to go and marry you, I've always got on quite well with the jocks, haven't I? But jocks is like everyone else, ain't they? There's your clever jocks — like old Matthew Whatshisname what only owns half of bleeding London — and there's your stupid jocks like the Soldier. I mean, it has to be said — he was a right mug!

19

CHARLEY I don't know as how you can say he's stupid, Harry. I mean, he fought . . .

HARRY Oh don't you? Well, you just listen to me for a minute or two — you might learn something. You ain't never been in the army, have you Charley?

CHARLEY No.

HARRY If you'd of been in the army, boy, you'd of known what I'm talking about! The Soldier was in the Scots Greys, right?

CHARLEY That's right.

HARRY And the Scots Greys is a jock regiment, right?

CHARLEY Yes, but . . .

HARRY No buts about it! The Scots Greys is a jock regiment! Every soldier knows that no jock what's got anything up here *(taps his temple)* ever signs up with a jock regiment!

SALLY Oh, Uncle Harry, don't be silly! What they got Scotch regiments for if Scotchmen ain't supposed to join them?

HARRY I didn't say that Scotchmen ain't supposed to join Scotch regiments, did I? What I said was — no *clever* jock ever signs up with a jock regiment!

SALLY But why not?

HARRY Why not? Your father came from Scotland and you ask me why not? All right, I'll tell you. Up in Scotland, they ain't a load of hairy bleeding cannibals like most of us English like to think — oh no! They've got schools, see? Parish schools. Every little nipper — and I mean *every* nipper, boy or girl, rich or poor, it don't signify — that comes off his mother's knee has to go to the parish school. So every little boy-jock and girl-jock what comes out of Bonnie Scotland can read, write and do arithmetic. They ain't like us pig-ignorant English, are they?

CHARLEY So what? I can read and write and do arithmetic!

HARRY Yes, but you ain't in the army, are you, mate? *(Pauses.)* Look at it this way, Charley. An educated bloke like you joins the army, right? Before you know it, you're a corporal, then a sergeant, then a master sergeant and — who knows — in time, you might even get to be an officer. That's in an

English regiment! Huh, you try it in a jock regiment and you've got no chance! Too much competition, see?

KATE   What's that got to do with the Soldier?

HARRY   Well, it stands to reason, don't it? I mean, if the Soldier had any savvy, he wouldn't of gone and joined one of his own regiments, would he? He'd have gone in an English mob, where the ranks is full of the scum of the earth and where they'd have handed him his corporal's stripes with his first fucking uniform! *(Exasperated.)* Jesus Christ! And you lot think you can run this country.

A short silence as HARRY *and* KATE *exchange glances.*

CHARLEY   You'd think he'd have know that, though. I mean, you'd think somebody would've told him about it.

HARRY   Know? Of course he knew! Stupid bloody jock, he's a mug, I'm telling you! A bleeding mug! *(Pauses.)* Mind you, that ain't taking anything away from what he did. He must be a very brave man and all *(with a slight degree of craftiness)* as I ought to know better than most!

KATE   *(in alarm)*   Charley! Don't say a word! Don't give him a chance to . . .

CHARLEY   How's that, then Harry? They give you the cat-o-nine-tails and all, then?

KATE   Oh God . . .

HARRY   What? Did they give me the cat-o-nine-tails? *(Laughs.)* You hear that, Kate? Did they give me the cat-o-nine-tails? No, sonny, they didn't give *me* no cat-o-nine tails! I was a Sergeant Farrier in the Hussars, wasn't I? I'm the bloke what had the job of handing it out!

CHARLEY   Oh!

HARRY   Yes. As a matter of fact, when I left the service . . .

HARRY *rises and goes to the cellar.* KATE *turns to* SALLY *with a groan.*

KATE   Oh dear! Here it comes! The Green Bag.

HARRY   . . . I held on to me old lash — just for a keep-sake, know what I mean?

HARRY *takes a green canvas bag from the dresser and lays it on the table. He takes a cat-o-nine-tails from it.*

HARRY   Here we are, then! The cat-o-nine tails! *(He shakes the lash on to* CHARLEY'S *lap.)* There you are, Charley — take a hold of one of them tails! Go on! (CHARLEY *does as instructed and* HARRY *pulls the lash taut.)* Right then, boy — how many knots can you see on that tail?

CHARLEY   Six.

HARRY   That's right — six. Six knots on every tail. Nine tails — cat-o-nine-tails so there must be nine tails, right? So — how many knots?

CHARLEY   Fifty-four.

HARRY   Each knot inflicts a wound — so that's fifty-four wounds per stroke! Multiply that by a hundred and see what you get!

CHARLEY   Five thousand, four hundred!

HARRY   A lot, ain't it? But that ain't all! Watch this!

HARRY *mimes a stroke, alarming* KATE.

KATE   Harry! Careful!

HARRY   All right, all right I know what I'm doing! *(To* CHARLEY.*)* Once you've made your stroke, you see you draw back the tails between your fingers — to get rid of any flesh or blood or skin or whatever — before you come on again. So it's all that much slower, know what I mean? In my time, I've done —what? Oh, must be at least thirty or forty floggings — and I ain't never seen a man take more than ten strokes of this *(indicates the lash)* without screaming his head off! Yet old Somerville the Soldier, he took a full hundred and never so much as opened his mouth! Not a word did he say!

KATE   That's as may be — but, if he comes in here and sees you standing with that thing in your hand I shouldn't wonder but that he'll have plenty to say!

22

HARRY Oh, all right — I'll put it away! I was only showing Charley, wasn't I?

HARRY *folds up the lash and puts both bag and lash back in the dresser.*

KATE You're always showing somebody that bloody whip! *(To the others.)* I believe he misses it, you know — handing out floggings to poor sods what don't know any better — give him a right sensation, it did!

SALLY It's horrible.

HARRY Horrible nothing, girl! It's discipline — the iron discipline of the British Army! It's what's made the British soldier what he is today!

HARRY *returns to his seat with something like triumph.*

CHARLEY That's right — a bloody slave!

KATE Hear, hear, Charley! Well said, son! Took the words right out of my mouth, you did!

HARRY A slave? What're you talking about, Charley Tyler? Listen, sonny-boy — if it weren't for the British soldier, you'd be a bleeding slave!

CHARLEY I ain't much better off now, am I? I ain't got much freedom, have I? I ain't got no rights!

HARRY Of course you have! What's the matter with you — of course you've got bloody rights!

CHARLEY No, I ain't, Harry! All I've got is the skill in them two hands! That's all I've got to bargain with — and some bargain it is, and all! Because I can't sell that skill at the price I want to sell it at can I? No chance, Harry! The Government controls the price. And who controls the Government? Not me, mate. I ain't got no vote!

KATE Hear, hear! You tell him, Charley!

CHARLEY Yet, for all of that, I'm still a damned sight better off than the poor bleeding British soldier, ain't I? At least, I can write a letter to the papers if I've a mind. At least I can think — and soldiers ain't allowed to do that! You ask Somerville when he gets here — he tried it, and look what happened to him!

HARRY (*huffily*) Bah, I don't know what's the matter with you lot! Two years ago, you were all shouting for Reform! Now you got it, you want something else! You ain't never satisfied — ask me, you're all barmy!

KATE Not as barmy as you are, you old hypocrite — not barmy enough to enjoy whipping a man with the cat-o-nine-tails!

HARRY What you talking about? Did I say I enjoyed it, did I? That's your trouble, Katie — all your life — you think everything's for pleasure! You want to enjoy everything! You don't seem to realise that . . . Oh Christ, here comes trouble!

Enter CAPTAIN GILLIES. *We can see by his clothes and his manner that he comes from a higher class than the others.* KATE *rises and greets him warmly.*

KATE Captain!

They take hands and GILLIES *kisses* KATE *on the cheek.*

GILLIES Evening Kate! Everybody! Sorry I'm late!

CHARLEY *and* SALLY *make noises of greeting.*

KATE That's all right, Captain. They ain't arrived yet — although we are expecting them at any minute. (*Smiles knowingly.*) Your usual, Captain?

GILLIES Thank you very much, Kate! I'll enjoy that.

KATE Sally — glass of claret for the Captain.

HARRY (*mimics*) Glass of claret for the Captain! (*Grumpily.*) How's about a glass of claret for the Sergeant, then? It's only his bloody claret when all's said and done!

GILLIES Hello, Harry! How are you?

HARRY No so dusty! All the better for knowing that you've pissed off, ain't I.

24

GILLIES It's not for long, Harry. I'll be back.
HARRY Will you? Well, don't hurry on my account!

GILLIES *smiles indulgently, turns to* CHARLEY.

GILLIES Hello there, Charley — good of you to come!
CHARLEY Well, it's my duty now, Captain!
GILLIES Good man! That's the spirit!

KATE *and* SALLY *pour glasses of claret and start handing them round.* KATE *takes one to* HARRY.

KATE There you are, you old sorehead — that ought to shut your moan!
HARRY Oh, thanks for nothing!

KATE *takes a glass for herself and resumes her seat.* GILLIES *takes up a place behind her and faces them all in a rather presidential manner.*

GILLIES Well, then! This is very cosy — very cosy indeed! I think perhaps . . .

KATE *holds her hand up.*

KATE Ssssh! Just a second, Captain! *(Listens.)* That sounds like . . .

Enter DUNCAN CRAIG, *followed by* SANDY SOMERVILLE. DUNCAN *is a short man, about thirty years of age, somewhat untidily dressed in a plain dark suit. A Glaswegian, he is normally persuasively talkative, but on this occasion he contents himself with a grin and a raising of his arm to indicate that he has brought the long-awaited visitor.* SOMERVILLE *is dressed in the same manner as* CRAIG, *but is much tidier. Long and thin — preferably the tallest member of the cast — he nonetheless communicates in his presence a certain strength. He looks much older than his twenty-three years and carries himself in a stiff-backed manner which is unmistakeably military. He*

25

holds a leather satchel bag. KATE *rises and approaches him in welcome, putting her glass down on the table.*

Welcome, welcome, welcome! Welcome to our humble abode, Mr Somerville! I'm Kate Barbour!

HARRY   Sally — glass of claret for the Private!

All laugh, except SOMERVILLE, *who looks a little bit bemused by his reception, glancing to* DUNCAN *for explanation, but getting none.* SALLY *has poured out two more glasses or claret and takes them to* SOMERVILLE *and* DUNCAN. SOMERVILLE *takes the glass, lays down the bag and steps further into the body of the room.*

GILLIES   I think, perhaps, since we all have our glasses charged . . .

KATE   That's the ticket, Captain — a toast!

GILLIES   Ladies and Gentlemen, I give you Somerville — Somerville the Soldier!

SOMERVILLE *is standing more or less in the middle of the room, with the others surrounding him. His eyes dart fiercely towards* GILLIES *as he speaks. When the toast has been drunk, they all wait expectantly for* SOMERVILLE *to make some kind of reply. Instead, he looks interestedly about the room, his eyes taking in everything, finally coming to rest on* GILLIES. *He raises his glass and points at* GILLIES.

SOMERVILLE   I ken your face!

GILLIES *(uncertain)*   I beg your pardon!

SOMERVILLE   I ken yer face! I've seen ye afore — somewhaur else!

GILLIES   Oh. Well, that's certainly not impossible! Very likely, in fact. We have many acquaintances in common, after all, and . . .

SOMERVILLE *snaps his fingers.*

SOMERVILLE   Hackney!

GILLIES Eh?

SOMERVILLE I was at a public dinner at Hackney — och, it wad be about echteen months syne. You were there.

GILLIES Was I? Oh, yes! Of course! So I was. *(Laughs.)* It wasn't a very good dinner, was it?

SOMERVILLE I wadna ken about that — it was the first public dinner I was ever at. Likely to be the last as well!

He takes a sip of his claret. The others watch him with something approaching fascination.

GILLIES You didn't enjoy it, then?

SOMERVILLE I went chiefly to hear a speech by Campbell the poet . . .

SALLY Thomas Campbell, you mean?

SOMERVILLE turns to her with interest and entirely without irony.

SOMERVILLE Is there anither Campbell that's a poet?

SALLY *(blushing)* No. No, I don't think so. I don't know much about poetry.

SOMERVILLE *returns his attention to* GILLIES.

SOMERVILLE I listened til the poet with intense interest. However . . . *(finishes his drink and lays it down carefully on the table)* I'm sorry to say that the pleisure I took in Mr Campbell's words was a wee thing marred. A group of gentlemen were sitting near at hand and . . .

GILLIES *(understands)* Oh!

SOMERVILLE It wad appear that a humorous story was being related. I canna mind the substance of the tale — but I mind fine the chiel that was telling it!

GILLIES Yes! *(Smiles with mock contrition.)* Oh dear! I suppose you thought that I was very rude?

SOMERVILLE Aye. I did.

Dismissively, SOMERVILLE *turns away from* GILLIES *and addresses* KATE.

27

Mistress Barbour, I hae nae wish to seem ill-mainnered myself, but I've had a lang journey . . .

KATE   Oh, of course! Sally, take Mr Somerville's bag and show him through to his room.

SALLY   Yes, Mum!

As SALLY *moves to obey,* SOMERVILLE *forestalls her, picking up his bag.*

SOMERVILLE   I'm no that weary, ma'am, that I canna manage my ain luggage!

SALLY   If you'd care to follow me, Mr Somerville.

SALLY *moves off to the right, followed by* SOMERVILLE. *At the door he stops and turns to address them all.*

SOMERVILLE   Well, then — I'll bid ye aa guid nicht!

KATE   Good night! But you'll join us later, won't you? Once you've . . .

SOMERVILLE   Thank ye, ma'am — but I fear I maun decline. *(Hesitates wearily.)* I'd hardly be fit company! Guid nicht wi ye aa.

SALLY   This way, Mr Somerville . . .

Exit SALLY, *followed by* SOMERVILLE.

KATE   Well! This is a fine how'd ye do and I must say! Here I am, worked hard all day to provide the best supper money can buy . . .

DUNCAN *comes forward to reassure her.*

DUNCAN   Just a second, Kate, just a second. *(Turns to take in the others.)* I think the rest of ye better listen to this and all! See, Sandy — well, he's no been right for a while, ye know? I don't know whether it's been the after-effects of his punishment — the flogging and that, ye know? — but he's no been himself.

28

CHARLEY Did you know him before, then, Duncan?

DUNCAN Well, no exactly — but I did meet him once or twice in Edinburgh, before he joined up. He was a different man then from the one ye saw the night — no question about it! Kate, I'm certain he didna mean to be rude or anything . . .

KATE Oh, I'm sure! It's just that . . . well, it seems such a shame, that's all!

GILLIES *goes to her.*

GILLIES I wouldn't worry too much about it if I were you, Kate! Your work won't be wasted — after all, the rest of us are here! *(Pause.)* Mind you, I must admit that his behaviour did seem rather strange!

HARRY Huh, I don't know about strange, Captain! He had your bloody number all right!

GILLIES Yes. I do seem to have offended his puritanical sensibility. What d'you think, Duncan? Is that going to harm us?

DUNCAN Well, it's no going to help, Captain.

KATE Well, help or hinder, it don't signify just now! Come on you lot — don't hang about like a bunch of crows at a duck's wedding! Let's go and have supper!

HARRY Katie, that's the first sensible thing you've said all night.

KATE *ushers them all out to the left.*

SCENE TWO

Tuesday morning. The wine and glasses have been cleared away and a tray with a teapot, cup and saucer and a plate of toast is on the table. HARRY *sits alone in his armchair, sucking at an unlit pipe and reading his paper.* SOMERVILLE *enters from the right and* HARRY *looks up.*

HARRY Morning, Jock! Sleep well, did you?

SOMERVILLE   Maister Hampden, is it?

HARRY   Oh, call me Harry, Jock, for goodness sake! No need to stand on ceremony with me, is there? Here, there's some breakfast there for you. Help yourself!

SOMERVILLE *goes to the table and starts to pour himself a cup of tea.*

Well, what you got on today, Jock? Any plans, have you?

SOMERVILLE *is irritated. He speaks with heavy sarcasm.*

SOMERVILLE   Were you addressing me, Maister Hampden?

HARRY *is surprised and puzzled.*

HARRY   Am I . . . Well, of course I'm addressing you, mate! Ain't nobody else here, is there?

SOMERVILLE   I thocht I heard ye speak til somebody cried Jock.

HARRY   So? I called you Jock. What's the matter with that? You're a . . .

SOMERVILLE *(severely)*   My name's no Jock, Maister Hampden!

This irritates HARRY. *He gets to his feet and goes to* SOMERVILLE.

HARRY   Listen to me, my lad — you and me better get something straight right off! You might be a big fucking hero to my sister and her loony friends, but you ain't nothing more than just another lodger to me! This is still my house and I still make the rules!

SOMERVILLE   And my name's still no Jock, Maister Hampden!

HARRY *throws his paper down on the chair in rage.*

HARRY   All right, all right, Mister Bleeding Somerville — will that suit you better? I was only trying to be friendly, wasn't I? *(Pauses.)* Look, I'll warn you, mate — I won't have anyone chucking their weight around with me! Not in here! So I'll have a little civility out of you, my lad — or, by Christ, I'll kick your arse out of here so fast your feet won't touch the ground! Now, do you understand that?

SOMERVILLE Aye. But I didna think it was me that was being uncivil, Maister Hampden.

In the face of such equanimity, HARRY *is speechless. His rage evaporates.*

HARRY Look, I'll tell you what I'll do with you, mate. Let's you and me strike a bargain — I won't call you Jock and don't you call me Mister Hampden. How's that?

SOMERVILLE *considers, then nods.* HARRY *extends his hand.*

HARRY Harry.

SOMERVILLE *takes his hand.*

SOMERVILLE Sandy.

They shake hands firmly. A trifle embarrassed, HARRY *turns away and resumes his seat.*

HARRY Right then — eh — Sandy. You'd best get on with your breakfast. I'll just sit here and read my paper. Don't worry — I won't disturb you. You just carry on.

There is a silence as SOMERVILLE *begins his breakfast and* HARRY *tries to read. The silence is too much for* HARRY, *however, and it is not long before he is folding his paper and addressing* SOMERVILLE *as if nothing had happened.*

HARRY Well, then! As I was saying, Sandy — what you got on today, mate?

31

SOMERVILLE Oh, I'm gaun til see a man about a job.

HARRY A job? what kind of job?

SOMERVILLE A newspaper job.

HARRY What — you mean, writing for the papers?

SOMERVILLE *gives a faint smile.*

SOMERVILLE Weill, I didna mean selling them!

HARRY *(laughs)* That your regular job, then?

SOMERVILLE No. No really. *(A little modestly.)* I'd like it to be, though.

HARRY Well, the best of luck to you, mate! I hope you get the job! Speaking for myself, I don't know much about newspapers — except for reading them, of course — and the only journalist I know is Duncan Craig *(with distaste)* and he's a right nerk, if you like!

SOMERVILLE How'd ye mean?

HARRY Oh, I'm sorry, Sandy. I suppose I shouldn't have said that what with him being a friend of yours and all!

SOMERVILLE Whae tellt ye that?

HARRY Eh?

SOMERVILLE Whae tellt ye Duncan Craig was a friend of mine?

HARRY Well, it was him brought you here, wasn't it? It was him got you to come down from Scotland— so I thought . . .

SOMERVILLE No! Naebody *brocht* me here!

HARRY What?

SOMERVILLE I was tired o Embra and I got the chance o this job in London — Fenchurch Street. I'd had dealings wi Duncan Craig afore and I reckoned he owed me something. So I wrote to him and asked if he could fix me up wi ludgins — that's aa!

HARRY Oh! Well, in that case, he's not just a right nerk — he's a first-class fucking chancer, that's what he is!

SOMERVILLE How'd ye mean?

HARRY Oh, I don't know — like as not I've got hold of the wrong end of the stick again. I'm always doing it. I thought that you and Craig knew each other.

32

SOMERVILLE Oh, I ken him aaright! That's no to say that he's my friend!

HARRY No. Well. *(Changes the subject.)* Anyway, tell me something, Sandy, will you? How'd you find it on Civvy Street?

SOMERVILLE Eh?

HARRY I don't suppose you miss the army.

SOMERVILLE Oh, I wadna say that. I was never better fed, claithed or quartered in my life. I'd jyne up again the morn, gin they gied me the chance. It's a guid life.

HARRY Ho, you're telling me, mate! Twenty years of it, I had, you know.

SOMERVILLE Oh aye?

HARRY Yes! Tell you the truth, I sometimes wonder why I ever bothered to come out! I mean, I thought — nice little pub, make myself a bit of money, a little bit of comfort, have something to show for my life, know what I mean? *(Grimaces.)* I didn't know my bleeding sister was going to move in did I? *(Pause.)* First-class regiment, the Greys, and all!

SOMERVILLE Aye! *(Pause.)* Mind you, gin I was to go into the airmy again, I wadna want to jyne a Scots Regiment!

HARRY No?

SOMERVILLE No, ye see, Scots Regiments are aaright — but aa the sodgers have been til the schule, ken their letters. English sodgers dinna get that chance — so ye've aye got a better chance o promotion in an English Regiment.

HARRY Now, it's funny you should say that, mate! It's very very funny you should say that. We were talking about that last night — yes, before you came in! 'Here' I says to Katie, 'here, I wonder what made an intelligent bloke like old Sandy Somerville go in a Scotch Regiment?' I mean, everybody knows that if a Scotchman's got any savvy, he's going to join up with an English mob — where they got all the scruff!

SOMERVILLE Weill, I wadna put it just like that!

HARRY Well — perhaps not. Still, why did you join the Greys, Sandy? Just as a matter of interest, like?

SOMERVILLE *(shrugs)* Nae option, Harry! I was out o work

33

C

and there was nothing for it but to take the shilling, as they say. The Greys was the only regiment handy.

HARRY   I was in the Hussars, myself! The Twelfth!

SOMERVILLE   Oh aye!

HARRY   Sergeant-Farrier I was!

SOMERVILLE   Ye'll ken aa about horses then?

HARRY   Oh, all there is to know, old son! All there is to know! *(Pauses carefully.)* Floggings and all.

SOMERVILLE   Aye!

HARRY   I've handed out a few lashes in my time, son. Believe me, I know a thing or two about what you had to suffer and . . .

SOMERVILLE *(brusque)*   Did ye ever take a flogging yourself?

HARRY   No, but . . .

SOMERVILLE   Then ye dinna ken! Ye canna hae the least idea!

HARRY   Oh, I wouldn't say that! I mean . . .

SOMERVILLE *(angry)*   Guid God, man! Gin ye kent ocht ava, ye'd ken that the last thing I want to do is talk about it!

HARRY *is chastened.*

HARRY   I'm sorry. I'm sorry. Didn't mean to upset you, did I?

SOMERVILLE   It's aaright.

HARRY   I mean, I just thought I'd let you know how much I admired . . .

SOMERVILLE *(angry)*   I'm telling ye — it's aaright!

HARRY   . . . what you done. *(Pauses, then rises, taking a pouch of tobacco from his pocket.)* Here, tell you what! Like a smoke, do you?

SOMERVILLE   Nou and then.

HARRY *approaches him with the pouch.*

HARRY   Here — cop a niff at this then!

SOMERVILLE *takes a smell at the pouch.*

SOMERVILLE   Guid stuff!

34

HARRY The best, mate! A pal of mine give it to me — he's in the trade, you see. Well, he ain't exactly a pal — more a sort of customer, really. Comes in the boozer. I do him the odd favour, he pays me back in kind, know what I mean? Want a fill?

SOMERVILLE Thank ye kindly — but I never smoke in the forenoon.

HARRY Well, suit yourself. Only, it's there whenever you want it, right? You only have to ask. Tell you what, the next time he comes in, I'll ask him to get you some. How's that, then?

SOMERVILLE Very kind of ye!

HARRY Oh, don't mention it, mate! No trouble! *(He puts the pouch back in his pocket and consults his pocket watch.)* Oh God! I'd best get on out of it! It's nearly opening time and I don't want a riot on my hands, do I? Fancy a pint?

SOMERVILLE *checks his own watch.*

SOMERVILLE No, I'll need to be watching the time myself! Maybe later on.

HARRY Well, if you get this job, you might want to celebrate, eh?

SOMERVILLE *(smiles)* Aye!

Enter DUNCAN *from the left, briskly.*

DUNCAN Morning, Sandy! How's it going? *(To* HARRY.*)* Aye, aye, auld yin! How's yourself?

HARRY *(coldly)* I'm all right, mate. *(To* SANDY.*)* See you, then, Sandy!

SOMERVILLE *nods to* HARRY *who exits left.*

DUNCAN What's the matter with him?

SOMERVILLE *rises and crosses to the right-hand chair. He sits down without a word.*

35

Sandy? (SOMERVILLE *gives him a look of disapproval.*) Did I say something or something? I mean, I generally get on all right with Harry, ye know. But that was one hell of a look he give me there! So what's the . . .

SOMERVILLE What's this ye've been telling these people?

DUNCAN Eh?

SOMERVILLE Ye ken what I mean! About me.

DUNCAN You? What're ye talking about?

SOMERVILLE What's this about you sending for me, bringing me doun to London?

DUNCAN Aw, I see! Well, listen, Sandy — I can explain that!

SOMERVILLE You better!

DUNCAN Look, it was a coincidence, that's aa! It just so happened that, at the time you wrote to me, they — that's to say, we — were looking for somebody like you!

SOMERVILLE What d'ye mean — somebody like me?

DUNCAN *hesitates, scratching his head.*

DUNCAN Look, Sandy, ye better let me start from the beginning, eh? (*Pauses.*) Ye ken about they lads from Dorset?

SOMERVILLE The Tolpuddle Six. Aye.

DUNCAN And ye ken that there's to be a big demonstration and march next Monday? Against their transportation?

SOMERVILLE Aye.

DUNCAN Well, there's a strong feeling in the Trade Union Movement that it'd be as well to have as many working-class leaders on the organising committee as possible.

SOMERVILLE So?

DUNCAN So they want you to join the committee! Walk at the head of the march with the rest of the leaders.

SOMERVILLE What?

DUNCAN That's what they want, Sandy!

SOMERVILLE It's impossible!

DUNCAN How's it important?

SOMERVILLE Working-class leader? Me?

DUNCAN Ye're well thought of, Sandy! Ye've got a guid name!

SOMERVILLE   Aye, and ye ken wha gied me that! *(Pauses, concerned.)* Listen, I canna jyne ony trade union committee.

DUNCAN   What for no?

SOMERVILLE   I'm no a member o a union! How can I be — I've no got a trade!

DUNCAN   Ach, that's no trouble! Ye can do what I did — join the General Workers! *(Hesitates.)* As a matter of fact, you're already a member.

SOMERVILLE   What? How can I be a member . . .

DUNCAN   I joined for ye. Last week.

SOMERVILLE *is hardly pleased but lets it go.*

SOMERVILLE   Oh, ye did, did ye?

DUNCAN   Aye, I kent ye wadna mind. And, I'm happy to say that at a meeting of the executive committee last week, it was unanimously decided to elect yourself as one of our representatives on the Tolpuddle March Committee. *(Pauses as* SOMERVILLE *gives him an outraged look.)* That is, of course, if ye agree to serve!

SOMERVILLE   Oh, I've got a choice, have I?

DUNCAN   Oh, of course! Listen, nobody's trying to rush ye into anything, Sandy! It's just that — well, time is of the essence and we had to get everything set up, know what I mean?

SOMERVILLE *lets it go with a nod.*

SOMERVILLE   I dinna ken. I mean, I'm no even shair that I agree with this demonstration!

DUNCAN   Ye support the Tolpuddle Six, do ye no?

SOMERVILLE   Oh, of course! I signed aa the petitions.

DUNCAN   Well then?

SOMERVILLE   It's tactics, Duncan, tactics. This demonstration's no gaun to do ony guid!

DUNCAN   I wadna say that! A wee show of strength — nothing wrong with that, ye ken!

SOMERVILLE   The Government'll be that busy worrying about a riot, they'll no take ony tent of the petition! I mean, fifty

37

thousand men marching through London . . . *(Shakes his head.)* Aside frae that, this Government's no gaun til budge! It daurna!

DUNCAN Well, that's a point of view right enough — but we have to try!

SOMERVILLE Aye! I suppose so!

DUNCAN Ye'll joint the committee, then?

SOMERVILLE *rises, scowling with concentration.*

SOMERVILLE Ach, Duncan . . .

DUNCAN We need ye, Sandy!

SOMERVILLE *(smiles)* That's a wee bit strange, is it no?

DUNCAN Not at all. The whole country kens that you're a man that'll no be stopped by trifles. Men like that are aye in short supply. We'll need every one we've got if we're to make a success of it next Monday!

SOMERVILLE *is suspicious.*

SOMERVILLE Make a success of what?

DUNCAN Ye ken what I mean.

Interested, SOMERVILLE *approaches* DUNCAN.

SOMERVILLE Duncan, this is mair nor a demonstration on Monday, is it no? There's something else.

DUNCAN There might be.

SOMERVILLE What?

DUNCAN I'm no in any position to say. *(Pauses.)* Look, I'll tell ye what: there's a committee meeting here the night. No the full committee, ye understand, just — well, a wee sort of sub-committee. Tyler, Gillies and myself — Kate Barbour'll likely be there as well. You join us, and we'll let ye have the whole story then, right?

SOMERVILLE Aaright!

DUNCAN *claps him on the shoulder.*

38

DUNCAN Guid lad, I kent ye wadna let us doun! Here, Harry'll have opened up the bar by this time — fancy a pint?

SOMERVILLE No, I'd better get away. I've an appointment with Nicholson.

DUNCAN Fenchurch Street? Aye, I heard that Cobbett had put ye up for a job with him! Dinna worry about it, son. Ye'll be aaright there!

Enter SALLY *from the left.*

SALLY Excuse me, gents, while I get Mr Somerville's tray. Here, I'm not interrupting anything private, am I?

DUNCAN No, it's all right, Sally. I was just leaving. See you later Sandy!

SOMERVILLE Aye, Duncan.

Exit DUNCAN *to the left.*

SALLY Oh, Mr Somerville! You haven't had your toast.

SOMERVILLE I'm sorry. I'm afraid I wasna hungry.

SOMERVILLE *turns to go to his room.* SALLY *takes a deep breath and starts to recite a poem which makes* SOMERVILLE *freeze.*

SALLY "My love, I see you as a light
fast in the forests of my night
a vision pure as pure moonbeam
that tells the truth in true delight.

My love, I see you as a stream
where crystals flash and shadows dream
whose waters wash so sweet and still
yet run far deeper than they seem.

As SALLY *recites,* SOMERVILLE *turns slowly, gazing at her in utter amazement.*

SALLY My love, I see you . . .

SOMERVILLE *holds his hand up.*

SOMERVILLE That's enough! *(Severely.)* Tell me, Miss Barbour
— are ye in the habit of making impromptu recitations?

SALLY I only wanted to let you know I knew it, that's all.
It's ever such a lovely poem.

SOMERVILLE That's no a poem — it's nothing but a daft bit of
verse!

SALLY That's not true! I think it's beautiful! I'll bet you
Thomas Campbell couldn't do any better.

SOMERVILLE It's guid of ye to say so — but that'll no alter the
fact that it's a piece o nonsense! I dinna ken why that paper
thocht to print it!

SALLY I'm glad they did — I'd never have known it otherwise.
(Pauses.) I know it's none of my business, but — well, did
you love her very much?

SOMERVILLE Eh?

SALLY The girl — the girl in the poem.

SOMERVILLE *is embarrassed.*

SOMERVILLE Miss Barbour, do I look the kind of man that's
in the habit of writing love poems to young girls?

SALLY But I thought . . .

SOMERVILLE Those verses were a feckless attempt by me to
describe my native district — the Lammermuirs! They fail
quite obviously to do so. And now, ye maun excuse me — guid
day to ye!

SOMERVILLE *turns to exit right.*

SALLY Mr Somerville!

SOMERVILLE Aye?

SALLY It don't matter what you say. It's still beautiful!

SOMERVILLE Aye, weill ye ken what they say about beauty,
Miss Barbour!

Exit SOMERVILLE.

40

SCENE THREE

Tuesday evening. Enter KATE, *followed by* CHARLEY.

KATE Come on, Charley! Give me a hand with this table!

CHARLEY Righto, Mrs B!

They pull the chairs away from the table, lift the table forward then re-arrange the chairs behind it. As CHARLEY *puts the last chair into place,* KATE *considers the arrangement with her finger to her lips.*

KATE Let's see now. Oh dear, we're one chair short!

CHARLEY Can I . .

KATE No, no, Charley! You stay where you are. I'll get one from Mr Somerville's room.

Exit KATE *right. Enter* GILLIES *left.*

CHARLEY Evening, Captain!

GILLIES Good evening, Charley! How are you?

They shake hands.

CHARLEY Can't complain, sir!

GILLIES Looking forward to Monday, are you?

CHARLEY Not half, sir! *(Hesitates.)* Do you think the Soldier's going to come?

GILLIES Don't see why not! That's what he's here for, after all! *(Carefully.)* You don't have doubts about him, do you?

CHARLEY Well, not exactly, sir. It's just that — well, he strikes me as a funny sort of cove, that's all!

GILLIES You've spoken to him, then?

CHARLEY No, sir — I haven't. Sally has, though — and Harry. From what they told me . . . well, he hardly seems the Revolutionary type!

GILLIES Revolutionary type, Charley?

41

CHARLEY You know what I mean, sir. Things he said, sentiments he expressed, so to speak — well, he don't seem to be the man we all thought he was, does he?

KATE *returns with a chair.*

KATE Who's not the man we thought he was?

KATE *puts the chair down in front of the table.*

GILLIES We are talking about Somerville, Kate. Charley was expressing some doubts about him!

CHARLEY Now, fair's fair, Captain — I didn't say doubts. He's probably all right, but — well, he did say some funny things!

KATE What things?

CHARLEY Well, for a start, he don't seem to hold any grudges against the army. Told Harry he'd join up again any time!

KATE Well, that's only natural, ain't it?

GILLIES Yes, it was the officers who punished him, Charley, not the men!

KATE He probably misses the company!

CHARLEY He don't strike me as the sort of bloke what needs much company, Mrs B. *(Continues.)* Then there's this business of religion . . .

KATE Religion?

CHARLEY Sally told me that he keeps three books at his bedside. One of them's the Bible and the others are religious books and all. A book of sermons and — what was the other one called? *(Thinks, snaps his fingers.)* "The Marrow of Modern Divinity" — that's it!

GILLIES *laughs.*

GILLIES Oh Charley! That's not religion, that's philosophy! A pretty crude form of philosophy, I must admit — but philosophy just the same. *(Explains to a puzzled* CHARLEY.*)* What you must remember, Charley, is that Somerville is a

Scot — and Scots don't go to church to worship, you know. They go to argue. The Scots love argument!

KATE You're telling me, Captain! You should've met my old man, Charley! Argue black was white, he would!

GILLIES Exactly! That's what makes them such excellent Revolutionaries! *(Claps* CHARLEY *on the back.)* So don't worry, Charley, don't worry! *(Smiles.)* In any case, you know, it doesn't really matter if Somerville goes with us all the way or not!

CHARLEY What d'you mean by that, Captain?

GILLIES Well, in a sense, Charley, it's not really Alexander Somerville we want, is it? I mean, what does the man have that's such an asset? A Lowland Scottish Labourer — that's all he is, really, you know — with the strong back of his class and the set determination of his race. We have plenty of the one — and more than enough of the other! No, it's not Alexander Somerville that we're interested in, Charley — it's Somerville the Soldier! He's a very different man!

KATE You mean all we want is his reputation? Surely he's worth more than that, Captain.

GILLIES Is he, Kate? I doubt it. That mob outside — the great mass of working-men, to whom you and I and Charley here have committed our interest — what do they know of Alexander Somerville? Nothing! They wouldn't as much as cross the street for him. But Somerville the Soldier? Ah now, that's different — they'd follow him through the gates of hell itself! *(Grins.)* In which case, they should have no difficulty in following him through the gates of St James's Park!

CHARLEY That's always providing he wants to lead!

GILLIES He'll lead, Charley. Never worry about that. As long as he takes part in the demonstration, as long as he's seen at the head of the march — they'll know and they'll follow.

CHARLEY Then why tell him anything at all?

GILLIES Oh Charley — I respect your doubts, but let's not be too pessimistic, eh? I believe that, given the chance, Somerville will come in with us. Duncan said that, when he thought that this was just another Trade Union do, he was very cool

43

— but once he guessed that there was something else afoot, he became very interested indeed!

KATE Well! Best wait and see what he says, eh? Are they going to be long, by the way? It's time we got started, you know.

GILLIES Yes — I told Duncan to keep him downstairs in the bar for a bit, so that we could — well, have the sort of conversation we've just had! *(Pause.)* Well, no point in standing about! They'll be up in a minute!

CHARLEY *and* GILLIES *take seats at the table.* KATE *takes a bound notebook from the dresser.*

GILLIES *(indicating the notebook)* Oh no, Kate! Not tonight! I don't think we ought to have anything in writing.

KATE But we have to have a minute!

GILLIES You can write it up later — when we know what's happened. Safer that way.

KATE Just as you please, Captain!

KATE *puts the book down and joins* CHARLEY *and* GILLIES *at the table. Enter* DUNCAN, *followed by* SOMERVILLE *from the left.*

GILLIES *(rises)* Ah, Somerville! Here you are at last! We've all been waiting! Come and sit down!

DUNCAN *takes a seat beside the others while* GILLIES *directs* SOMERVILLE *to the chair in front of the table.* GILLIES *sits down with a smile.*

GILLIES Well! Let me say straightaway how delighted we were when Duncan told us you'd be joining us tonight!

KATE Yes, Mr Somerville — it's a very great honour to have you with us!

SOMERVILLE *(patient)* Thank ye ma'am.

GILLIES Somerville, I'll come to the point soon enough — but let me first of all ask you a question. What's your opinion of this present Government?

SOMERVILLE *is guarded.*

SOMERVILLE I did my share in the Movement for Reform — so I suppose I canna make owre muckle o a complaint if it's no turned out the way we aa thocht it wad.

GILLIES You feel betrayed?

SOMERVILLE Disappointed wad be a better word.

GILLIES Oh, Somerville — let's speak frankly! This Government has shown itself to be totally insensitive and, indeed, highly inimicable to the wishes of those who elected it. In short, as a populist Government, pretending to be based on the principles of the Reform Movement, it is nothing more than a sham!

DUNCAN That's right!

KATE Hear! Hear!

CHARLEY *raps on the table.*

GILLIES What new and sweeping measures has it undertaken? Eh? It has reformed the Irish Clergy — thereby putting one million into the already overburdened coffers of the spiritual tyrants of Ireland. It has reformed the administration of the Bank of England, the Court of Chancery, the East India Company. All well and good — if you happen to be even a moderately rich man. Most of us, however, are anything but rich — many of us are poor, very poor. And, towards the poor, this Government has shown itself in its true colours!

CHARLEY *(nodding)* The emancipation of the West Indian slaves!

GILLIES Exactly, Charley! When the Government introduced a bill which proposed a payment of twenty million pounds to the owners of the West Indian slave plantations, it was cheered to the rafters by that gang of religious philanthropists and philosophical liberals in the House of Commons! A bargain for humanity it was called.

DUNCAN I was a bargain aaright! A bargain for the slave-owners!

GILLIES A free gift to the bosses! As for the millions of hard-working men and women of this country, the Government

45

made their attitude plain enough when they arrested the Tolpuddle Six! Six working men tried to raise the level of their wages to a point where they could live as well as any slave — and the Government responded by sentencing them to seven years transportation each!

KATE We'd be slaves ourselves — slaves and worse than slaves — if we allow our brothers in the union to be transported!

SOMERVILLE I ken that. I signed the petition.

GILLIES Petitions aren't enough, Somerville — not any more! As we see it, the working-classes of this country have only two choices open to them. They can either initiate another long struggle for the reform of the Constitution — a struggle which would last years without any guarantee of real success and which wouldn't help the Tolpuddle Six in the slightest — or they can follow the example of the French and drive straight for a People's Government here and now.

GILLIES *pauses, left breathless by his own passion and in any case unwilling to go further without some sort of response from* SOMERVILLE. *The others watch expectantly as* SOMERVILLE *rises slowly, absently drawing his pipe from his pocket. He turns away from them all, fiddling with his pipe, a frown of concentration on his face.*

SOMERVILLE Revolution, ye mean?

CHARLEY That's right, mate! Revolution!

GILLIES *moves quickly to* SOMERVILLE.

GILLIES Monday's march from Copenhagen Fields will be nothing more than a cover! The Prime Minister will meet us, accept the petition, then expect us to disperse peacefully. *(Shakes his head.)* When we get to Downing Street, Somerville, peace will be the last thing on our mind!

KATE We'll take the Prime Minister prisoner and occupy Number Ten!

GILLIES But that will only be a diversion — to draw the troops from the barracks at St James's Park!

46

DUNCAN   Aye! When the army rides to the rescue, three hundred of our own men will launch an attack on the barracks!

SOMERVILLE   Three hundred?

CHARLEY   Three hundred of the best democrats in England! Hand-picked men from Birmingham, Sheffield, Nottingham, Glasgow.

DUNCAN   The boldest and the best! Street-warfare veterans from the Continent an aa! Frenchmen, Poles, the bravest lads in the world for an enterprise like this!

Emotionally, GILLIES *puts his hand on* SOMERVILLE'S *shoulder.*

GILLIES   But we want the bravest lad of all to lead them! Somerville, what do you say?

Embarrassed by GILLIES' *touch,* SOMERVILLE *breaks from him.*

SOMERVILLE   What happens after the Barracks are taken?

CHARLEY   We arm the rest of the workers of course!

KATE   We take over the Government and all its functions — Downing Street, Whitehall, the House of Commons!

DUNCAN   The banks. Dinna forget the banks!

CHARLEY   We'll arm the rest of the workers and by evening the city will be ours!

SOMERVILLE   And what if the workers wilna consent to be armed?

GILLIES   They will — once they know that Somerville the Soldier's in command!

SOMERVILLE *takes this with a philosophical sigh.*

SOMERVILLE   I've nae battle experience, ye ken that?

GILLIES   You've been trained to fight, haven't you?

SOMERVILLE   I've been trained to ride a horse, use a sword and a pistol. Maistly though, I've been trained to dae what I'm tellt! I haenna the first idea of command!

CHARLEY   That don't signify! It's your name we're interested in — not your abilities!

GILLIES *(reproves)* Charley!

SOMERVILLE My name? Is that aa I'm worth til ye?

GILLIES It's a great deal, Somerville. Your name, your reputation, it's the best possible weapon we can get. What do you say, man? Are you with us?

SOMERVILLE *hesitates.*

SOMERVILLE I dinna ken. I'll need to think about this.

DUNCAN Och, come on, Sandy! Dinna be sae blate, man!

SOMERVILLE *(angry)* I've no aye been blate, Duncan. *(Pauses.)* I'll need to think about it — aye, and I'll need to ken a bit mair of whae I'm dealing with here! *(Nods.)* I'll hae to let ye know.

CHARLEY Oh no! Sorry, Mr Somerville — but I ain't having that! We've been honest with you, haven't we? Put our cards on the table, told you all our plans. We've laid ourselves wide open to betrayal!

SOMERVILLE I'll gie ye my word of honour no to betray ye!

CHARLEY That ain't good enough.

SOMERVILLE What for no? My word's as guid as ony man's here!

CHARLEY If I'm arrested for high treason, your word of honour ain't going to do me any good, is it?

GILLIES Charley's right, Somerville. One way or the other, we need to know now. Are you with us or not?

SOMERVILLE *considers.*

SOMERVILLE In that case, aa I can say is . . .

Enter HARRY, *urgently, from the left.*

HARRY Sorry to break in, gents — but this is important.

KATE Oh Harry, what is it?

HARRY Sandy, you got visitors, old son. Couple of gents waiting downstairs.

48

GILLIES   Can't they wait?
HARRY   Afraid not, Captain. It's the law.

All except SOMERVILLE *exchange glances.* SOMERVILLE *pockets his pipe, buttons his jacket and goes to the door.*

SOMERVILLE   Mistress Barbour, Gentlemen — I fear ye maun excuse me!
GILLIES   Somerville!

SOMERVILLE *turns slowly, smiles.*

SOMERVILLE   Dinna fash yourself, Captain. I tellt ye my word's as guid as ony man's here!

Exit SOMERVILLE, *followed by* HARRY. *The others sit down wearily.*

SCENE FOUR

Much later that evening. KATE *is sitting alone at the table, writing in a bound notebook. She hears a sound and looks up warily, laying down her pen.* SOMERVILLE *enters from the left, looking all in.*

KATE   Oh, Mr Somerville! What have they done to you?
SOMERVILLE   Whaur are the ithers?
KATE   Oh, they've gone — ages ago! We weren't expecting you back tonight, you see!

SOMERVILLE *pulls back a chair and sits.*

What did they want?
SOMERVILLE   Och, nocht to speak about! *(Rubs his chin.)* Listen, have ye got a drink?

49

D

KATE A drink? Oh! Yes, of course, What you want — whisky?
I got some whisky.

SOMERVILLE Fine!

KATE *goes to the dresser and takes out a bottle of whisky and
a glass, thinks, then takes out another glass.*

KATE What was it all about then?

SOMERVILLE Eh?

KATE They must have pulled you in for something!

SOMERVILLE Oh, the Law, you mean! *(Shakes his head.)* It was
nothing. They wanted to ken what brocht me to London,
that's aa!

KATE The sauce! I hope you told them to mind their own
business!

SOMERVILLE Words to that effect, Mistress Barbour, words
to that effect.

KATE *pours out two glasses and hands one to* SOMERVILLE.

KATE There you are, then! You get outside that and you'll feel
a lot better!

SOMERVILLE Thank ye kindly!

As SOMERVILLE *drinks,* KATE *picks up her own glass and considers him.*

KATE Mind if I ask you something, Sandy? You don't mind if
I call you Sandy, do you?

SOMERVILLE *shakes his head.*

How old are you?

SOMERVILLE *smiles.*

SOMERVILLE Twenty three.

50

KATE Twenty three! Is that all? *(Smiling, she shakes her head and sits down.)*

SOMERVILLE What's the matter?

KATE Oh nothing — it just seems to me that a young fellow your age ain't got no business always being so solemn and serious about everything.

SOMERVILLE I wasna aye sae serious.

KATE Perhaps not — but you certainly are now! I mean, look at you, Sandy! Sitting there — all buttoned up in your clothes! You want to relax a bit more, mate! Put your feet up! *(Pauses.)* I mean, you might take your jacket off for a start! Eh?

SOMERVILLE *hesitates, looks at her, shrugs. He rises, takes his jacket off and drapes it over the back of his chair.*

KATE That's better! *(Finishes her drink.)* Drink up and we'll have another! *(She rises and goes for the bottle.)* I mean, you've got to have some fun while you're young, ain't you? Else when you going to have it? That's what I always say! *(Pours out a drink for herself.)* Twenty three, eh? *(Laughs.)* I wish I was twenty three again, Sandy, I can tell you! *(Goes to* SOMERVILLE *and fills his glass.)* Oooh, you should have seen me then, love! Popular I was, very very popular — oh, not like you are, of course, but popular enough! Men loved me, Sandy, when I was twenty three — lots and lots of men. *(Giggles.)* At least, they said they did — and I was never one to argue! *(She sits down again.)* But you know what? Men had far less reason to love me then than they have to love you now.

SOMERVILLE How d'ye make that out?

KATE *(laughs)* If I have to tell you that, my boy, then I really am getting old!

SOMERVILLE Ach, ye're hardly auld, Mistress Barbour!

KATE Well, I must say, *Mister Somerville,* that's very gallant of you — very gallant indeed! There you go again, Sandy — all buttoned up in your clothes! Mistress Barbour! For God's

51

sake, Sandy, call me Kate like everyone else! Mistress Barbour sounds like a character in a bleeding play! *(More seriously, as* SOMERVILLE *does not respond.)* So. The police only wanted to talk to you did they?

SOMERVILLE Aye.

KATE Do that often, do they?

SOMERVILLE Often enough.

KATE Why?

SOMERVILLE *(smiles)* Did ye no ken? I'm meant to be a dangerous man!

KATE *(careful)* You don't think they know anything, do you?

SOMERVILLE What about?

KATE You know! About what we were talking about tonight?

SOMERVILLE I didna tell them — if that's what ye mean.

KATE Oh, of course not, stupid! But someone might have talked mightn't they? You don't suppose they've heard a rumour . . .

SOMERVILLE *shakes his head.*

SOMERVILLE I couldna say.

KATE What did they ask you?

SOMERVILLE I tellt ye! They wanted to ken my business in London.

KATE And what did you tell them?

SOMERVILLE The truth. *(Pauses.)* I'm looking for work.

KATE And they didn't ask you anything else?

SOMERVILLE *(smiles)* They took lang aneuch to ask me onything ava! (KATE *looks puzzled.)* It's called harrassment, Kate. They want me to ken I'm no forgotten.

KATE Oh, I see. *(Pauses.)* You know, Sandy, you're a lot different from what I thought you'd be.

SOMERVILLE Disappointed, are ye?

KATE Now why should I be disappointed?

SOMERVILLE *(laughs)* Maist folk seem to think I should be riding around on a white charger, dressed up til the nines in a fancy uniform! They're aye that let doun when they find out I'm just a common sort of lad!

KATE Tell me, Sandy — why'd you do it?

SOMERVILLE Do what?

KATE You know what I mean!

SOMERVILLE Oh! That business in Birmingham, eh?

KATE Yes.

SOMERVILLE *rises and, for lack of anything else to do — he is nervous of the turn the conversation is taking — picks up the bottle and pours another drink.*

SOMERVILLE Ye wadna understand.

KATE *holds out her glass.*

KATE Well, you might give me half a chance!

SOMERVILLE *pours some whisky into her glass. He does not respond and* KATE *considers her drink for a moment.*

I mean you must have known — when you wrote that letter — that it was going to get you into trouble.

SOMERVILLE Oh aye? And how wad I ken that?

KATE Oh Sandy, come on! *(Quotes.)* 'The Scots Greys will be the last to degrade themselves below the dignity of British soldiers, in acting as the tools of the tyrant. The Duke of Wellington, if he sees or hears of this, may assure himself that military government shall never again be set up in this country.' God love you, boy, if that ain't a seditious letter, I don't know what is!

SOMERVILLE *(sharply)* Hou can it be seditious to defend the Constitution? Aa sodgers hae a duty til do that!

KATE That's as may be, Sandy — but the authorities didn't see it that way, did they? *(Pauses.)* What happened, boy? They haul you up in front of the C.O. straight off, did they?

SOMERVILLE No!

KATE Whyever not? I should think your commanding officer had a blue fit! God, it wasn't the sort of thing he could just leave alone, was it? I mean, it must have made some sort of impression on him! I know it made one almighty impression on *me! (Pauses, more evenly.)* Sandy, I can't tell you the effect that letter hard on me when I read it first. God, I thought, what a man that Somerville must be! What a bold, courageous, determined honourable hero of a man, to dare to put his signature to a letter like that!

SOMERVILLE It was anonymous.

KATE What?

SOMERVILLE Anonymous. When it first appeared in the *Birmingham Weekly,* the letter was unsigned.

KATE Oh! *(Slightly deflated, she quickly recovers.)* Then how on earth did they know it was you what wrote it?

SOMERVILLE They didna. As a maitter of fact, they thocht it was anither chiel aathegither.

KATE But they found out that it was you?

SOMERVILLE Ah aye! I wasna gaun til let onybody else suffer for ocht that I'd done — so I tellt them.

KATE What? You mean you owned up — turned yourself in?

SOMERVILLE No exactly. I just let it be known that it was me that wrote the letter.

KATE Well! That's marvellous, I must say! That's bleeding marvellous! You mean to tell me that you admitted it — you admitted writing that letter?

SOMERVILLE Well, I wasna ashamed of it, Kate!

KATE Of course not! But . . . well, don't you see, Sandy? If you'd kept mum about the whole thing . . .

SOMERVILLE I couldna do that!

KATE Why not?

SOMERVILLE They'd have flogged the other lad, that's why. They'd have flogged an innocent man!

KATE But they couldn't do that! I mean, if he was innocent, the Court Martial would've acquitted him!

SOMERVILLE *is amazed.*

SOMERVILLE Och!

KATE What's the matter?

SOMERVILLE Listen, Kate, there was nothing illegal in what I did. D'ye understand? There's nocht in King's Regulations that says a sodger canna write to the papers if he has a mind. Aa I did was to put into writing what every man in that garrison felt — when they herded us into the barracks, denied us visitors, drilled us on the Sabbath, gart us roch-shairpen our swords so's we'd have guid effective weapons for dealing with a civil mob. Oh, we kent what was coming aaright — and it was me that made the protest! But the thing is, there was no way that they could put me on a charge for it! *(Pauses, then as* KATE *looks none the wiser.)* I wasna court-martialled and I wasna flogged for writing to the papers!

KATE Then why . . .

SOMERVILLE They gave me a horse that naebody else could ride. I couldnae ride it either. I refused to try.

KATE You were victimised? It was a trumped up charge?

SOMERVILLE That's it!

KATE *rises and moves towards him.*

KATE You were given a hundred lashes for a trumped-up charge?

SOMERVILLE Two hundred was the sentence. *(Smiles grimly.)* They let me off with the second hundred.

He is standing with his back to her.

KATE Sandy, was it very . . .

He turns and their eyes meet.

SOMERVILLE Aye!

KATE *(nervously)* Harry said — well, he said there'd be wounds, lots and lots of wounds. Thousands.

SOMERVILLE *nods a trifle wearily.*

55

I suppose — you've got scars, then? Thousands of scars — on your back?

SOMERVILLE I've got scars.

KATE *hesitates, breathlessly.*

KATE Sandy, will you . . .
SOMERVILLE Eh?
KATE Show me! Show me, Sandy! Show me your scars — please!

SOMERVILLE *looks away uncertainly.*

SOMERVILLE What for?

KATE *moves very close to him.*

KATE Let me see them, Sandy! Please. Let me see your scars!

SOMERVILLE *goes to the table, hesitates, then lays down his glass. Slowly, he unbuttons his shirt and removes it completely.* KATE *gasps as she sees the mass of scars across his shoulder blades and down his back. Gingerly, she reaches out to touch them.*

Oh! You poor boy! You poor, poor boy!

She runs her hands over his scarred skin, slips her hands under his arms and embraces him as she puts her mouth to his wounds.

SCENE FIVE

Five days later, Sunday afternoon. HARRY *and* SOMERVILLE *are seated at the table, playing draughts. They each have a half-drunk glass of beer by them and a number of empty beer bottles are on the table.*

HARRY I don't know! I don't know! Where'd you learn to play this game, mate?

HARRY *makes his move, taking two men, and leaning back in triumph.* SOMERVILLE *responds with another move, which takes four men, leaving* HARRY *gasping.*

SOMERVILLE Crown him!

HARRY Why, you crafty . . .

HARRY *crowns* SOMERVILLE'S *man reluctantly and considers his next move. Since* SOMERVILLE *has torn his game apart, there isn't a great deal he can do and he tries to start a conversation.*

Here — are you going to be fit enough to go on this march tomorrow?

SOMERVILLE Play the game, Harry!

HARRY I mean, you have been ill haven't you? You've been laid up in bed for the last three days. Nobody can blame you if you call off now!

SOMERVILLE I said — will ye play the game!

HARRY Only — from what I've heard — it could turn out to be a bit of a dodgy do!

SOMERVILLE Harry, wad ye please make your move!

HARRY Oh, all right! *(He moves one of his men and sits back.)* Had a couple of union blokes in last night, didn't I?

SOMERVILLE Oh aye.

HARRY Bakers, they were. They reckoned — the mood their members were in — that we might be in for some fun tomorrow.

SOMERVILLE Fun?

HARRY Yes! You know what I mean — a riot. Like that business at Coldbath Fields last year — when the bobbie got knifed.

SOMERVILLE I'd hardly call that fun!

HARRY Well — just a manner of speaking, ain't it? Mind you I'm not saying that some people I could mention — not a thousand miles away from here either — wouldn't find it enjoyable to start something like that. My sister Kate, now — bloodthirsty bitch, she is, always has been! Do you know that . . .

57

SOMERVILLE *moves a man.*

SOMERVILLE Your move, Harry.
HARRY Oh, sod it!

HARRY *makes another move.*

Anyway, I'm going to piss off out of it, ain't I?
SOMERVILLE Are ye?
HARRY I've got a mate lives over Croydon way. George Tanner
— good bloke, we was in the service together. I'm going to
shut up shop for the day and go and see George.

SOMERVILLE *moves a man.*

Look here, Sandy — why don't you come with me, eh? You'd
like George! He's a good bloke, like I say, and you and him
. . .
SOMERVILLE Listen, are you playing this game or are ye no?

HARRY *bangs the table in anger.*

HARRY Damn you, Somerville! Damn you! Bloody man, you
ain't been listening to a word I've said, have you?
SOMERVILLE I thocht we were supposed to be playing a game
. . .

HARRY *turns the board over.*

HARRY Sod the game! *(Gives a glance over his shoulder.)*
Listen, mate, I'll leave off beating about the bush and give
it to you proper! I know what's happening tomorrow, you
know!
SOMERVILLE Do ye?

SOMERVILLE *straightens the board and begins to arrange the
pieces, setting up another game.*

58

HARRY Of course I do! I ain't a fool, you know. I ain't deaf neither! Uprising! What do they know about organising an uprising! They're all barmy, I'm telling you, they're all off their bleeding rockers! It can't work, Sandy, it can't . . . Look, would you stop doing that!

HARRY *upsets the board again.*

You're going to listen to me whether you like it or not!

SOMERVILLE *(calmly)* Aaright. I'm listening.

HARRY *gives another glance over his shoulder.*

HARRY Like I said, this uprising, this so-called Revolution — it's barmy, it won't work! Oh, I daresay they might be able to get their hands on a few guns — they might even be able to take London. But how long are they going to hold it, eh? A day, two days, a week? Sandy, you know the British Army better than that! Do yourself a favour, mate — stay well out of it!

SOMERVILLE Is that aa? Are ye finished?

HARRY Look, why don't you come to Croydon with me, eh? See George? The three of us can make a day of it — get pissed as arseholes together. What d'you say?

Enter DUNCAN. SOMERVILLE *looks up at him.*

SOMERVILLE I'm sorry, Harry. I've got plans for the morn.

HARRY Sandy, you . . . *(Notices* DUNCAN.*)* Oh, hello, Craig!

DUNCAN Hello there, Harry! How's yourself?

HARRY I've been better.

DUNCAN Sandy? Keeping better, are ye? Got over your bad turn.

SOMERVILLE Aye. I'm aaright nou, Duncan.

DUNCAN Fighting fit, eh? Ready for the *(glance at* HARRY*)* march the morrow?

SOMERVILLE *drains his glass of beer.*

SOMERVILLE   Any chance of anither bottle, Harry?

HARRY   I suppose so! *(Rises.)* I expect you want one and all, Craig?

DUNCAN   Well, I wouldn't mind, Harry, ye know.

HARRY *picks up the empties.*

HARRY   Righto, then! Hang about!

Exit HARRY *to the left.*

DUNCAN   Here, Sandy, what's the matter with the auld fella, eh? Have ye any idea what I've done to upset him?

SOMERVILLE   Maybe he just doesna like Glaswegians.

DUNCAN   I got on well enough with him before! Whatever it is, he certainly seems to have taken a scunner at me! *(Brightens.)* Still, never mind, eh? *(*SOMERVILLE *rises and* DUNCAN *dances up to him like a shadow boxer.)* The morn's the morn, eh? The morn's the day we're gaun til hand a bloody nose til the tyrant! Man, Sandy, it's grand to see ye back on your pins again!

SOMERVILLE *smiles and moves away from him.*

Here, ye will be fit for the morn, will ye no?

SOMERVILLE *turns to look at him.*

SOMERVILLE   Duncan, ye're trying to use me again, is that no right?

DUNCAN   Use ye?

SOMERVILLE   Aye. Like ye did after the court-martial.

DUNCAN   What're ye talking about?

SOMERVILLE   Oh, Duncan, D'ye no mind? Ye wrote to me when I was in hospital, speired for the haill story. I replied with what I thocht was a private letter to a friend. Ye published that letter in geynear every paper in the country!

DUNCAN So what? I didna do ye any harm, did it?

SOMERVILLE *turns away again.*

SOMERVILLE Duncan, a few days ago, I went for a job.

DUNCAN Oh aye! With Nicholson — how'd ye get on?

SOMERVILLE Oh, he'll employ me aaright! He'll even put a weekly column in the paper with my name at the heid o't!

DUNCAN Great!

SOMERVILLE The only thing is — he'll no let me *write* the column!

DUNCAN What?

SOMERVILLE Aa he wants is my name! It'll sell a few thousand copies for him — he says. *(Laughs.)* Somerville the Soldier! Ye want to ken something, Duncan? I dinna even pronounce my name that way! Sandy Simerel, that's me, no Somerville! I loathe Somerville, Duncan, ye ken that? I detest him. He's no a man ava — just a twisted representation of something I did aince. And it was you that did the twisting, Duncan, it was you!

DUNCAN Oh, Sandy, come on — be fair!

SOMERVILLE Aye, aye, I ken! It wasna just you! There were ithers as well. But that hardly alters the facts o't!

DUNCAN Others? Aye, there were others! Others making fortunes for themselves; There was one fella — I canna mind his name the now, but he stopped in every pub atween here and Birmingham collecting donations for ye! You didna see a penny o't though, did ye? I could have done that, Sandy, I could have done that easy! Instead I spent aa my time and the maist of my energy agitating to get you a Court of Inquiry!

SOMERVILLE Aye, because it suited ye! I didna ask ye to do it!

DUNCAN Oh, ye're an ungrateful bastard, Somerville! You made two hundred and fifty quid out of that Court of Inquiry — a Court of Inquiry that I helped to make for ye! Ye wadna hae gotten a penny without me!

61

SOMERVILLE I micht hae got mair!

DUNCAN Wad ye . . .

SOMERVILLE What price do you put on justice, Duncan? Eh? Because that's what I was after when I put in for the Court of Inquiry — justice!

DUNCAN Well, ye got justice, did ye no? Two hundred and fifty quid's worth of justice!

SOMERVILLE No! No, Duncan — justice was the last thing I got! If you and your friends in the press had left it alane, I micht hae had a chance of getting the man that victimised me — Major Wyndham —punished for what he did! As it was, half my evidence was inadmissible, I couldna state my case properly and Major Wyndham . . . Major Wyndham's Lieutenant-Colonel Wyndham nou! That's the punishment he got — he was promoted!

DUNCAN Well, ye can hardly blame me for that, Sandy!

SOMERVILLE It was you and your kind made aa the publicity, Duncan! Whae else do I blame?

Enter CHARLEY *from the left. He takes in the situation and frowns.*

CHARLEY What's all this then?

DUNCAN Hello, Charley! Ach, it's him — he doesna ken whae his friends are, that's his trouble.

DUNCAN *sits down on* HARRY'S *armchair.*

CHARLEY What's the bother, Somerville?

SOMERVILLE Forget it, son. It's nothing to do with you.

CHARLEY *bristles at the use of the term 'son'.*

CHARLEY Listen, Somerville — we're going to be relying on you tomorrow. At least, some of us are. So if you've got a moan, I think we've all got a right to know what it is.

DUNCAN Ye'll never believe it, Charley. He thinks we're using him.

CHARLEY Using him? *(Approaches* SOMERVILLE.*)* That's right. We're using you — you're being used. I'm being used. Duncan's being used. Mrs B, the Captain, they're being used and all! We're all being used, Somerville! Fifty thousand workers are being used! So what's so special about you? Why shouldn't you be used?

SOMERVILLE Every man's special to himself. Every man's entitled to keep his ain counsel.

CHARLEY *and* DUNCAN *exchange troubled looks.*

CHARLEY Here — you ain't backing out, are you?

DUNCAN *rises.*

DUNCAN Aye, ye're still wi us, Sandy, are ye no? Ye'll no let us doun? We're aa counting on ye, ye ken!

SOMERVILLE That's kind of daft, is it no, Duncan? I've been in my bed for the best pairt of a week . . .

CHARLEY He is! Damn him, he's trying to back out!

DUNCAN No, Sandy! Ye canna, man!

SOMERVILLE Canna what, Duncan? I never promised . . .

Furious, CHARLEY *bears down on* SOMERVILLE.

CHARLEY Listen, mate, I don't care what you say now! You gave us your word of honour and . . .

SOMERVILLE I said nocht about . . .

CHARLEY You gave us your word of honour and you're bloody well going to keep it! I don't care if you don't strike a single blessed blow, you're going to march with these men tomorrow if I have to drag you there myself!

CHARLEY *seizes* SOMERVILLE *by the lapels.* SOMERVILLE *calmly takes* CHARLEY'S *wrists and slowly but surely twists his hands away. Enter* HARRY *from the left, with a jug of beer and some glasses on a tray. He lays the tray down on the table as he sees them.*

HARRY   Here — what the . . .

With a sudden movement, SOMERVILLE *sends* CHARLEY *staggering away from him across the room. As* CHARLEY *tries a fresh assault on* SOMERVILLE, HARRY *intercepts him.*

HARRY   Wait a minute, Charley! What d'you think you're doing?

CHARLEY   It's his fault, Harry! He's a bloody . . .

SOMERVILLE   You started it, son!

DUNCAN *(to* SANDY*)*   I thocht you were supposed to be no weill!

SOMERVILLE   I'm aye weill aneuch to look to myself!

HARRY *(shouting)*   Hang about, hang about, hang about! Where the hell do you lot think you are then, eh? *(He gets silence.)* What kind of house do you think this is? I'm warning you, if any of you are looking for a punch-up, you can have it out in the street — not in here! Not in my house! I ain't going to have any bloody brawling in here understand? *(Pauses.)* Now, then — let's hear it. What's the bother?

DUNCAN   Ach, it was nothing, Harry! A wee argument about the march, that's aa. Charley got kind of carried away!

HARRY   Charley?

CHARLEY   Yes, that's right, Harry. I got carried away. Sorry.

HARRY   Yes — well, you want to watch it, boy. You make any more trouble in my house, you'll get carried away for good, understand?

CHARLEY   I said I was sorry, Harry!

HARRY *is about to make further comment but changes his mind.*

HARRY   Oh, all right! Let's forget it and have some beer! There ain't any more bottles — so I brought a jug up. Sit down, the lot of you! *(He notices that* DUNCAN *is about to return to his armchair.)* Not there, Craig! *(Indicates a seat at the table.)* Here!

CHARLEY *and* DUNCAN *take seats at the table while* SANDY *sits*

64

down on the right-hand armchair. HARRY *pours out beer as he talks and hands it round.*

Speaking for myself, it beats me why you're having this march in the first place.

CHARLEY It's for the Tolpuddle Six.

HARRY Well, I know that much you fool! What I mean is — what good d'you think this march is going to do? The government ain't going to shift just because a bunch of scruff go walking down the street, are they? Besides, I don't see what it's got to do with you lot; a bunch of bleeding yokels down Dorset decide to break the law — well, they got to be punished, haven't they? I mean, if you're going to start having demonstrations and marches for every bleeder what breaks the law, where's it all going to end then, eh?

The beer dispensed, HARRY *assumes his favourite chair.*

DUNCAN Ach, ye dinna understand, Harry. It's no a question o folk breaking the law!

HARRY Them Tolpuddle blokes, they got a fair trial, didn't they?

DUNCAN Oh, sure! As fair as possible, but . . .

HARRY Well then! If they got a fair trial and were found guilty, then they broke the law! Stands to reason! They broke the law and they got to be punished! Serves them fucking right, ask me!

CHARLEY It's a question of liberty, Harry — individual liberty.

HARRY Oh, I see! People ought to have the liberty to break the law, is that it?

CHARLEY *(sighs)* The Tolpuddle Six combined into an organsiation — a trade union — to negotiate for better pay and conditions. If that's against the law, Harry . . .

HARRY Well, if it ain't against the law, mate, why the hell are they transporting them?

DUNCAN It's what ye call a test case, Harry. The ruling classes ken fine that if they can make this sentence stick against they

65

E

Dorset lads, then they've created a precedent. They can use the same charge owre and owre again, move against the bakers, the tailors, the carpenters, the general workers! There'll be no stopping them! No working-man's organsiation'll be safe — this is the thin end of the wedge that this government means to drive atween the working-classes to destroy the trade union movement!

CHARLEY That's it, Duncan!

HARRY Bloody good thing too, ask me!

CHARLEY What!

HARRY Come off it, Charley — what's the good of the trade union to the average bloke, eh? I mean, it's only bleeding trouble-makers and malcontents like you lot what get any benefit from it! I mean, look at it this way, mate — you're in the carpenter's union, ain't you? You're a carpenter?

CHARLEY That's right.

HARRY Well, nobody's asking you to be a carpenter, are they? Nobody's forcing you! If you don't like it or you ain't happy with the money they give you, why don't you piss off and get another job?

CHARLEY How about that, then, Duncan? Marie Bleeding Antoinette!

DUNCAN Aye. Let them eat cake. What an attitude!

HARRY Well, you may not like it, Craig — but that's the way things are! Talk about your individual liberty! Listen, if them blokes from Dorset wasn't happy down on the farm, why the hell didn't they just pack their bags and come up to town? There's plenty of work for them here! They could have told the farmer to stuff it, couldn't they? (*Pauses, turns to* SOMER-VILLE.) You're very quiet, Sandy — ain't you got nothing to say about this? I mean, you used to work on a farm, didn't you?

SOMERVILLE Aye. I've wrocht on a fairm.

HARRY Well, then — you tell them about it.

SOMERVILLE *sips his beer, smiles.*

SOMERVILLE What d'ye want me to say, Harry? That you're

richt and they're wrang? *(Shakes his head.)* I canna do that! Ye see, I ken aa about the Tolpuddle Six — I've been whaur they've been. At the hairst, at the pleuch, in the stables — hedging, ditching, stane-breaking, wood-sawing. And my faither did it aa afore me — still does it. It's slavery, nocht but slavery. Some fairmers treat their hands waur nor they treat their beasts. My faither's wage this year is less nor it was last — he's aulder, ye see, and as far as the fairmer's concerned, worth less. *(Pauses with a sigh.)* I could never thole the thocht o sic a life — I left the land as soon as I was able. I was entitled to do that — on the other hand, gin I'd wanted it, I'd hae been entitled to bide anaa! A man can only work at what he's fit for, Harry — and, gin that richt's denied him, what else can he do but fecht for it?

HARRY Then you support them yokels?

SMERVILLE I'm a yokel myself, Harry.

HARRY And you'll go with them on this march tomorrow?

SOMERVILLE *stands up and drinks his beer.*

SOMERVILLE Whatever happens the morn, Harry, has got nocht to do with Tolpuddle. That struggle was about liberty — tomorrow is about power. Duncan's admitted it — the big union's are feared!

DUNCAN I never said that!

SOMERVILLE They're terrified that they'll be next — as well they micht! *(Puts his glass down on the table.)* Whatever happens, the Tolpuddle lads are Australia-bound — and aa the marches in creation winna bring them back!

SOMERVILLE *moves to the right.* CHARLEY *stands up.*

CHARLEY Somerville!

SOMERVILLE *turns.*

I was right, wasn't I? You're backing out!

SOMERVILLE Whae tellt ye I was ever in?

Exit SOMERVILLE *to the right.* CHARLEY *and* DUNCAN *exchange anxious looks.*

HARRY Well, lads — it looks like you've lost him, don't it?

Without a word to HARRY, CHARLEY *and* DUNCAN *exit hurriedly.* HARRY *gets up and goes to the table.*

HARRY Don't it just?

He raises his glass and toasts in the direction of SOMERVILLE'S *bedroom.*

SCENE   SIX

Late Monday morning. Enter KATE *from the left, dressed for the street. She goes directly to the right and exits.*

KATE *(off)* Sandy? Sandy?

Enter GILLIES. *He waits for* KATE *to re-enter, which she does.*

He ain't there! His bed ain't been slept in!
GILLIES I know.
KATE Where the hell's he got to then? I mean, time's getting on, Captain! We ought to get started shortly or . . .
GILLIES He won't be coming, Kate.
KATE What?
GILLIES Somerville won't be coming. I very much doubt if we'll ever see him again.
KATE Don't talk daft, Captain! All his things are there, his bag, his books, his . . . *(A thought strikes her.)* Here! He's not been had by the Runners again, has he? The law hasn't
. . .

68

GILLIES *shakes his head.*

GILLIES   No, no, no, Kate — nothing like that! As far as I know, he's quite free.

KATE   Then why do you say . . .

GILLIES   He's just not interested, Kate. Doesn't want to know!

KATE   Doesn't want to . . . but he can't do that! We was counting on him! The whole Working-Class Movement was counting on him! He can't walk out now, he can't . . .

GILLIES   I'm telling you, Kate, He doesn't want to know.

KATE   He said as much himself, has he?

GILLIES   In so many words. He told Charley and Duncan yesterday afternoon . . .

KATE   Yesterday *afternoon!*

GILLIES   I didn't tell you, Kate, because I knew you'd be upset and . . . well, I thought that I could talk to him, get him to change his mind.

KATE   And did you? Talk to him, I mean.

GILLIES   He was gone before I had the chance. I doubt that I would have been successful in any case. He's not the kind of man who changes his mind easily.

KATE   I don't believe this! I just don't believe this! He's Somerville the Soldier, for God's sake! He stood up for the working-classes once — and, from what I've seen of him, he's not the man to be afraid to do it again. *(Pauses, grasps at a straw of hope.)* I'll tell you what! He's gone on ahead of us, that's it! Yes, I'll wager any money you like, Captain, that when we get to Copenhagen Fields, Sandy'll be waiting for us! He won't let us down, Captain, I just know he won't!

GILLIES *goes to her, taking her firmly by the shoulders.*

GILLIES   Look, Kate, we've got to face up to this! It's a great blow to our hopes, I know, but we have to face it — Somerville has deserted us! He's not coming back, Kate! He's never coming back.

As GILLIES *is talking,* SOMERVILLE *enters from the left.* KATE
sees him over GILLIES' *shoulder, breaks from* GILLIES *and runs
to embrace* SOMERVILLE.

KATE Sandy! Sandy! I knew you wouldn't let us down, I just
knew it! *(Turns to* GILLIES.*)* You see, Captain! I told you
he'd be back. Now, we'd best all get started! We've wasted
enough time already and . . .

GILLIES You go on ahead, Kate! Somerville and I have things
to talk about.

KATE Well, you can talk on the way, can't you? I mean, they'll
be waiting for us down Copenhagen and . . .

SOMERVILLE Better do like he says, Kate.

KATE *seems about to voice suspicions, but thinks better of it.
She glances from one to other of them, then gathers herself
to leave.*

KATE All right then! Only don't take all bloody day about it,
will you? We've got a Revolution to win!

Exit KATE *left.* SOMERVILLE *ignores* GILLIES *and begins to move
right, towards the right exit.*

GILLIES Kate thinks very highly of you, Somerville. She's going
to be very . . . *For God's sake, man! Stand still when I'm
talking to you!*

SOMERVILLE *halts, then turns with a half-smile to face* GILLIES.

GILLIES Don't you dare walk away from me! *(Approaches*
SOMERVILLE.*)* Somerville, you're behaving like a damned fool!
You know that, don't you? Eh?

SOMERVILLE *sighs and shakes his head.*

SOMERVILLE Ach, Gillies . . .

70

SOMERVILLE *turns away again. Gillies seizes him by the shoulder and turns him round.*

GILLIES I *said* — don't you dare walk away from me!
SOMERVILLE Weill, what d'ye want?
GILLIES You know what I want.
SOMERVILLE No chance!

GILLIES *turns away from the confrontation.*

GILLIES Then I only hope that you're prepared to pay the penalty, that's all!
SOMERVILLE Dinna think ye can scare me, Gillies.
GILLIES Scare you? My God, I should think you'd be scared! I'll tell you this: if I were in your shoes I'd be terrified! *(Points at* SOMERVILLE.*)* Fifty thousand men, Somerville — fifty *thousand* — are gathered today on Copenhagen Fields! It is their prime intention to pull this system of government down to the ground and slit its throat! You have chosen to desert them — so do you think they're going to have any qualms about slitting yours?

SOMERVILLE *shakes his head.*

SOMERVILLE Ye dinna ken muckle o working folk, do ye, Gillies?
GILLIES Oh, don't give me that, Somerville! For God's sake, don't think you can flash your proletarian credentials at me! In the eyes of your extremely limited experience I may seem like a pretty fine gentleman — but I can assure you that I come from a background every bit as humble as your own.
SOMERVILLE Oh, do ye now, *Captain* Gillies?
GILLIES Yes, I do! I grew up in a room half the size of this — with my mother and my father and seven brothers! I fought for my position, Somerville — right up through the ranks, every inch of the way! So don't you dare sneer at my rank — it was earned! And don't you think that I've forgotten the black hole that I've crawled out of — or of the thousands

that languish in it yet! *(Pauses.)* Not that that makes a jot of difference to you.

SOMERVILLE Aye. Richt aneuch. I still say ye dinna ken muckle o working folk!

GILLIES You don't believe me! Good God, man, what do you want? That I should show you my callouses?

SOMERVILLE *smiles, shakes his head, walks reflectively across the room.*

SOMERVILLE Fifty thousand men, ye say?

GILLIES More or less.

SOMERVILLE Aa united wi ae common purpose — to pull doun the Reform Government and create a true democracy, a People's Government?

GILLIES That's right!

SOMERVILLE *looks hard at* GILLIES.

SOMERVILLE Then I suppose William Lovett kens aa about this, does he?

GILLIES *is guarded.*

GILLIES Lovett? What do you know of William Lovett?

SOMERVILLE I was at his house yestreen. I slept the nicht there.

GILLIES Lovett doesn't know anything about our plans. This has nothing to do with him!

SOMERVILLE *nods.*

SOMERVILLE I see. Then how about Frank Place? Does he ken?

GILLIES Frank Place! Of course not! Place is a government spy — everybody knows that!

SOMERVILLE Oh aye! Do they? Then how about Cobbett, Hume, O'Connor — how about Robert Owen?

GILLIES Robert Owen is a boss! A better boss than most I grant you, but a boss no less! Look, Somerville, what is this? Why

72

do you keep throwing these names at me? What are you driving at?

SOMERVILLE It strikes me as unco strange, Captain, that you can organise the workers o this country for revolution without saying a word to their leaders!

GILLIES These men are *not* their leaders!

SOMERVILLE Oh, are they no?

GILLIES Not their true leaders!

SOMERVILLE Oh aye! And who is? You? Kate Barbour? Duncan Craig? Somerville the Soldier? Are you seriously trying to tell me that fifty thousand working men'll follow me afore they'll follow William Lovett or Robert Owen?

GILLIES Not them all, no! But the vanguard will!

SOMERVILLE The Vanguard! Oh aye, the famous Vanguard — your three hundred hand-picked democrats! Your Frenchmen and your Poles! *(Pauses.)* You're a military man, Gillies — ye ken as weill as I do that ye canna take St James's Park Barracks wi three hundred men!

GILLIES It's possible. With the right leadership . . .

SOMERVILLE Come off it, Gillies! Ye're no talking to Katie Barbour nou! It's no possible to take Oxford Street wi three hundred men! *(Shakes his head.)* Oh, dinna you worry, Captain — I ken your game!

GILLIES What do you mean?

SOMERVILLE Ye gang about the public-houses and ye hob-nob wi union cast-offs and radical misfits — hot-heids like Chairlie Tyler and lunatics like Craig. Ye mak grand speeches at public meetings — say aa the richt words in the richt places — ye scrieve articles in radical journals, publish seditious pamphlets! Oh aye, ye're the braw hero richt aneuch! But ony man wi that much *(snaps his fingers)* common sense can see what you're at, Gillies! Gin the working classes speir at you for justice, they'll be a lang while speiring! *(Scoffs.)* Fifty thousand men! You've no got fifty thousand — I jalouse ye've a lot less than the three hundred ye claim . . .

GILLIES I have a lot more than . . .

SOMERVILLE But even if ye *have* got three hundred, they're

73

three hundred mugs! Weill, Gillies, this is one mug ye'll no get! I wadna forfeit my life for a single second to serve the ambition o your insane dreams!

GILLIES I've already told you, Somerville. Your life is forfeit in any case.

SOMERVILLE Aye weill, I'll tell you what, Captain. Away you go and get aa the bloodied heids ye want — and, gin that doesna satisfy ye, come and look for mine. I'll no be hard to find.

GILLIES I can see that I've over-estimated you, Somerville. I thought you'd understand our struggle.

SOMERVILLE Oh, I understand aaright!

GILLIES *shakes his head.*

GILLIES No, you don't. You accuse me of dreaming of power — very well. I plead guilty to the accusation. Politics is about power, Somerville. After today, whatever happens, no government of this country will be able to ignore the power of the common people — they'll have no choice but to deal with it!

SOMERVILLE Aye, and its so-called representatives, I expect?

GILLIES That's right.

SOMERVILLE And what about the People's Government, eh? The New Jerusalem ye promised to Kate and Chairlie and the rest of them?

GILLIES *laughs.*

GILLIES Oh, Somerville! You really don't understand, do you? These people are idealists — yet I'll tell you this: if they thought for a moment that the struggle was to be long and the eventual goal distant, they wouldn't raise a finger to help. Still, in their way they're useful enough. They're pioneers, they smooth the way for the more practical men among us. Without such people, mankind would barely have emerged from barbarism.

74

SOMERVILLE Gillies, I swear that you're the maist barbarous rogue that it's ever been my bad luck to meet!

GILLIES *smiles good-naturedly.*

GILLIES Oh, I know you've never liked me, Somerville — you made that plain from the first. But that doesn't matter. I stand for progress and the future. You might have had a place in history, but you had to turn it down. Very well. I'll leave you to your obscurity. *(Moves left.)* Only — don't be here when I return tonight, will you? I strongly advise against it.

SOMERVILLE And what if I am?

GILLIES *(smiles)* Then I'll see you in hell, Somerville. That's what. I'll see you in hell.

Exit GILLIES *left.*

SOMERVILLE Hmm. No me, Captain. No if I see you first!

Exit SOMERVILLE *right.*

SCENE SEVEN

Two hours later. Noises off : The sound of drumbeats, marching feet, the jingle and clatter of cavalry. SALLY *enters hurriedly from the left, wearing a shawl and bonnet and carrying a shopping basket.*

SALLY *(calling)* Sandy! Sandy! Come quick, come quick!

Enter SOMERVILLE *from the right. He is in his shirtsleeves and has a towel about his neck. He moves to* SALLY *to calm her.*

Sandy, the streets is full of soldiers! Thousands and thousands of soldiers! They're heading for the . . .

75

SOMERVILLE *(soothingly)* Aye, aye, I ken! But it's aaright! They're no gaun til . . .

SALLY *clutches his hands.*

SALLY But they're heading for the march, Sandy! All them soldiers — what they need all them soldiers for . . .

SOMERVILLE Shush, shush, shush! There's nae need for you to get upset, Sallyl! I'm telling ye!

SALLY But Mum's at the march — and Charley and Duncan and the Captain! What they going to do, Sandy? Is there . . .

SOMERVILLE Listen, Sally . . .

SALLY Is there going to be fighting, Sandy? Tell me! Is there? Mum and the rest of them . . . Oh, what's happening, Sandy? What's happening?

SOMERVILLE *shakes her by the shoulders.*

SOMERVILLE Get a grip on yourself, lassie! Get a grip on yourself! *(Kinder.)* I'll explain aathing gin ye'll just gie me the chance! Nou, come on, sit doun there . . .

SALLY But Sandy . . .

SOMERVILLE Sit doun, I'm telling ye! I'll explain it aa to ye!

He leads her to HARRY'S *armchair. She sits down, pulling a handkerchief from her sleeve. As she dabs at her eyes,* SOMERVILLE *pulls up a chair and sits beside her.*

Now then — the first thing is that naebody's gaun til get hurt. The sodgers'll see to that — that's what they're there for.

They hear the sound of distant cannon.

SALLY What's that?

SOMERVILLE It's aaright, Sally. It's just the Artillery letting aabody ken they've arrived.

SALLY   The Artillery? Oh, I don't understand!

SOMERVILLE   Look, Sally — your mither and her friends were gaun til try and do something that was — weill, gey stupid to say the least. In fact, it's that daft, I hardly ken how to tell you about it!

SALLY   What was it?

SOMERVILLE   Ye'll never believe this . . . they were gaun til kidnap the Prime Minister.

SALLY   What?

SOMERVILLE   Aye! Start a Revolution by their way o't! Crazy, but weill, an awfy lot o folk could have got hurt, maybe even killed! Still, it's aa sorted now. They'll no even get the chance to make a fool o themselves.

SALLY   How do you know?

SOMERVILLE   Never mind. I ken — just you trust me and leave it at that!

SALLY   But how can I be sure . . .

SOMERVILLE   Listen, when your mither gets hame, I'll tell ye the whole story. How's that?

SALLY   She will be safe, then?

SOMERVILLE   Oh aye!

SALLY   You sure?

SOMERVILLE *nods.* SALLY *sighs.*

She's always going on about Revolution — but, well I never took her seriously, did I? I mean, I thought she was just — well, you know — making up.

SOMERVILLE   How'd ye mean?

SALLY   Well, you know! Making up for something you ain't got, something you miss. *(Explains.)* I mean, when Mum was young, she was very nice-looking, wasn't she? Had all them young fellows running after her. Then, she met me Dad — and he didn't half give her a dog's life, I can tell you! *(Confesses.)* A bit of a sot, me Dad was, you know.

SOMERVILLE   Oh aye?

SALLY *(nods)* He was a Scotchman, like you — or rather *not*

77

like you. He wasn't like you at all! He was carpenter to trade, came from a place called Dunfermline — it's in Fifeshire.

SOMERVILLE Aye, I ken Dunfermline! What was a jyner frae Dunfermline doing in London?

SALLY Getting sloshed, mostly. That's what killed him, as a matter of fact.

SOMERVILLE Oh dear. Died of drink, did he?

SALLY No! He wasn't that much of a sot! Only, he was playing cards one night at the old Cock's Feathers in Camberwell — that's where we used to live, Camberwell. He'd had a skinful as usual and, as he was leaving, he fell down the stairs — broke his neck. *(Pauses sadly.)* I was only twelve at the time, wasn't I? Anyway, it was after that that Mum started to get involved in this Reform business — really threw herself into it, she did. She was making up, you see? She missed me Dad and she didn't have all them men chasing after her — so she had to have something, didn't she?

SOMERVILLE I see what ye mean. And then the Reform Bill was passed.

SALLY Yes. So I suppose she had to have something else. When she started going on about Revolution, I thought . . . well, I never thought there was any harm in it. I just thought that . . . *(The significance of it strikes her.)* Oh, my God! Revolution! What do we want with Revolution, for God's sake? We're all right as we are!

SOMERVILLE *smiles and rises, walks a few steps away.*

SOMERVILLE I only wish it was that simple, lassie.

SALLY What d'you mean?

SOMERVILLE Weill, ye dinna think that this was your mither's idea, do ye?

SALLY You mean someone talked her into it?

SOMERVILLE Of course!

SALLY But what for? I mean, why Mum? If they really wanted a Revolution, surely . . .

The logic of her reasoning remains unspoken.

SOMERVILLE Exactly.

SALLY Oh my God!

SALLY *rises in fright and goes to* SOMERVILLE *who takes her by the shoulders.*

SOMERVILLE But it's aaright nou, Sally! I'm telling ye, it's aa been sorted. So ye're no to worry, ye hear. *(SALLY has bowed her head with concern and he lifts up her chin.)* Promise me ye'll no worry.

SALLY I'll try not to, Sandy — but it won't be easy.

SOMERVILLE It never is, lass — it's no meant to be.

She turns from him and resumes her seat.

SALLY Oh Sandy! How I wish I could be like you!

SOMERVILLE Like me?

She reaches for his hand and grips it tightly.

SALLY Hard and strong and brave.

SOMERVILLE Brave? *(He smiles, pats her hand and drops it, turning away from her.)* Ken this, Sally? It's easier to be brave than maist folk think. *(She gives him a sceptical look.)* D'ye no believe me?.

SALLY Well, it's all right for you to say! I mean, everybody knows what you did at Birmingham . . .

SOMERVILLE Oh, Birmingham, Birmingham! Will I ever be free of Birmingham?

SALLY Well, you did a brave thing there, Sandy. Don't try to tell me different!

SOMERVILLE *smiles.*

SOMERVILLE Courage never comes on its lane, Sally.

79

SALLY How d'you mean?

SOMERVILLE Afore a man can be brave, he maun be feart or angry or determined as weill. Oh, I kept my courage at Birmingham richt aneuch — but that was because I was angry. Angry at the injustice of it aa, angry because the Maister Sergeant tellt me that he'd let me off gin I'd just get doun on my knees and beg! Huh, what d'ye think of that — me, a British sodger and I'm supposed to beg! *(Shakes his head.)* But what really got my dander up was the man they chose to flog me. Farrier Simpson — my best friend.

SALLY What?

SOMERVILLE Aye. The best friend I had in the world — and they tellt him to put a lash to my back! Puir Simpson! It maun hae been a sair trial for him.

SALLY But couldn't he have made it easier? Couldn't he have . . .

SOMERVILLE *silences her with a shake of his head.*

SOMERVILLE His first stroke caught me just ablow the neck — I felt a stound that gaed aa the way doun to my toenails and across to my fingers. It stung me to the hert as if a knife had gane into my body! I heard a voice cry *'One'* and I prayed to God that he wadna catch me in the same place again. The second was a wee bit lower and, compared to that, I thocht the first had been sweet and agreeable. The third caught me on the right shoulder and the fourth on the left. They were bitter aneuch, but the fifth was even worse. It was queer — the time atween ilka stroke seemed that long, yet the next stroke aye came owre soon. As the lash fell, the Sergeant Major cried out the number and I tried to occupy myself by doing mental arithmatic. When he came to 'twenty-five' I thocht, that's an eighth — I've got seven times mair of this to thole. *(Pauses, remembering.)* After the twenty-fifth stroke, they stopped and Simpson had a bit rest. They replaced him wi this young trumpeter — I kent him anaa, but no as weill as Simpson — and he'd never flogged a man afore this. Still, he'd had plenty practice on stable posts and sacks o sawdust, so he kent what he was at. He was very scientific. He gied me a guid rowth o cuts about the ribs, but that didna seem to please them, because I heard somebody tell him to hit me higher up — which he did. The pain on my back by this time was bad aneuch, but inside me it was worse — I felt as if my lungs were like to burst. I think I must have ruptured something because my mouth started to fill up wi bluid. I felt myself start to groan wi the pain, but I'd sworn I'd die afore I'd do that, so I put my tongue atween my teeth and geynear bit it in twa. What wi the bluid frae my lungs and the bluid frae my tongue, I aamaist choked, so the doctor come up wi a drink o water for me. I pulled back my heid and spat out the bluid. He could keep his water — I wasna gaun til gie in til him or onybody else! *(Pauses again.)* After fifty, the trumpeter stood aside and Simpson came on again — heavier this time and, I thocht, slower. He'd no hae the stomach for the job puir chiel, so I cried out to him 'Come quicker on, Simpson, and let it be done! You are very slow!' I dinna ken if he got quicker after that or no — aa the lashes seem to take owre lang to me. *(Pause.)* It was when the trumpeter was near the end o his second twenty-five — ninety-four or ninety-five, in the nineties anyway — that my anger began to fade and I thocht maybe I should yield, beg forgiveness. The thocht had hardly entered my heid when the anger flared up again. 'Na, na, na!' I thocht 'never will I beg to them!' At last, I heard the voice o Wyndham, the commanding officer 'Stop' he says 'He's a young sodger! Cut him doun!' So they cut me doun and led me awa to the hospital. Even then, my anger hadna abated — I swore I'd get them back for what they'd done to me!

SALLY And you did, didn't you?

SOMERVILLE *shakes his head.*

SALLY But the Court of Inquiry . . .

SOMERVILLE *laughs.*

F

SOMERVILLE The Court of Inquiry gied me money and a discharge — I wanted neither. I got neither justice nor revenge — no that that maittered by then. Ye see, Sally, an even greater trial was to come — and aa the courage and anger in the world couldna see me through it.

SALLY What was that?

SOMERVILLE D'ye mind thon poem?

SALLY 'My love, I see you as a light'?

SOMERVILLE Aye. I tellt ye that that was about the Lammermuirs — that's no true.

SALLY It *was* about a girl — I knew it!

SOMERVILLE *nods.*

SOMERVILLE Sally, gin I had my way, d'ye ken whaur I'd be nou, eh? In a fairm-cottage in the Lammermuirs, working as hird or a pleuchman. The lassie in thon poem wad be my wife — and mair nor likely we'd have had twa - three bairns by this time.

SALLY What happened, Sandy — she turn you down?

SOMERVILLE No exactly — but she didna accept me either. She micht hae mairried me — gin it wasna for aa the clash there'd been about the flogging. I'd drawn attention to myself, ye see, and she didna like that.

SALLY What? Wasn't she proud of what you did?

SOMERVILLE No proud aneuch to mairry me.

SALLY She was a fool!

SOMERVILLE *smiles and nods.*

SOMERVILLE Maybe she was — but I'd still gie my richt airm to mairry her. (*Laughs bitterly.*) Queer, is it no? Your mither canna thole the thocht o a humdrum life here wi you and your uncle Harry — so she makes up for it by getting herself talked into a Revolution. Me, I'm a walking Revolution — yet I'd do anything to be back ahint a pleuch in the Lammermuirs wi her waiting for me at the hous. (*Shakes his head.*) How do I make up for that, Sally?

82

SALLY *rises and goes to him.*

SALLY You don't have to make up for anything, mate! *(Pauses.)*
People live boring lives, Sandy, and that's a fact. Most people
anyway. There ain't no excitement in them, no adventure.
But we all like to think that somehow, somewhere, someone
is doing something — wonderful. Yes, that's it — wonderful.
Something that we can all wonder at. Something we can all
share in. *(Smiles.)* A young soldier defies his officers and
writes a letter to the papers — ain't that just the thing that
most people want to do? Tell the boss or the wife or the
husband or the parent to get knotted? The officers take the
young soldier and punish him — now, ain't that the very
thing that stops them doing what they want? But what does
this young soldier do, eh? He don't take their punishment —
at least, he don't accept it. They give him the cat-o-nine-tails
— a hundred strokes — and he don't scream or cry out for
mercy! Not once! Now that ain't what his officers had in
mind, is it?

SOMERVILLE Sally, I tellt ye — it wasna because I was brave.
It was because I was angry!

SALLY *shakes her head fiercely.*

SALLY It don't matter, Sandy! It don't matter why you didn't
cry out — the fact is you didn't! And because you didn't,
you put a little bit of excitement into the lives of thousands
of ordinary people. Whether you like it or not, mate — you're
a hero! Charley Tyler saw you once — sitting next to his
Uncle Stan — and just seeing you, and being part of the
crowd that was cheering you, gave Charley a night that he'll
never forget for as long as he lives. Somerville the Soldier!
Hurrah!

*In the distance, the sound of cannon is heard again. Im-
mediately frightened,* SALLY *throws herself into* SOMERVILLE'S
arms and clings to him.

Sandy! What's happening now? Why are they firing again?

SOMERVILLE It's aaright, Sally. It's aa finished nou. Your mither'll soon be hame.

SCENE EIGHT

About an hour later DUNCAN, CHARLEY *and* KATE *troop in wearily.* DUNCAN *slumps down on* HARRY'S *armchair,* CHARLEY *pulls up a chair at the table, while* KATE *goes to the dresser and takes out the bottle of whisky and three glasses. She splashes a generous quantity of whisky into each one and silently hands them out. She goes to her own armchair and sits down wearily. They all drink gratefully.*

KATE God! What happened! What went wrong?

CHARLEY Somebody opened his gate!

KATE *(irritably)* Well, of course somebody opened his bleeding gate, Charley! That's obvious, ain't it? The question is — who?

DUNCAN Could have been anybody, Kate. I mean, there was plenty knew the plan. Too many, I'd say.

CHARLEY Yes, but they was all sworn to secrecy, wasn't they?

DUNCAN *(laughs)* So what? That wadna mean much if one o them was a government spy to begin with, wat it?

KATE Is that what you reckon, Duncan? A spy?

DUNCAN *sighs and shakes his head.*

DUNCAN I dunno. I mean, it looks that way right enough, but . . . well, there's something gey twisted about this!

CHARLEY How's that, Duncan?

DUNCAN Well, if the government kent our plan — what for did they no make any arrests?

KATE Maybe they did.

84

DUNCAN How d'ye mean?

KATE Well, we ain't seen the Captain for a while, have we?

DUNCAN *shakes his head.*

DUNCAN No, Kate, no chance! If they'd picked up the Captain, they'd have picked up the rest of us. I dunno where the Captain's got to, but I hardly think he's been arrested. Anyway, that's no the point. The thing is, if the government kent our plans, they could have done anything they liked with us. Ambushed our men in the barracks, had troops hiding in Number Ten — it could have been Cato Street and the 1820 Rising all over again. They could've wiped us out!

KATE Oh, maybe they just wanted to keep it all quiet!

DUNCAN In that case, what for did they no arrest us aa last night? That wad've been quiet enough, wad it no?

CHARLEY Maybe they didn't know our names.

DUNCAN *(laughs)* Ye're joking! If they kent our plans, Charley, they kent our names — no mistake about that, as Harry wad say!

KATE Then maybe they didn't know!

DUNCAN They knew something, Kate — no mistake about that either. Strikes me we were lucky the day. *(A thought strikes him.)* Or maybe no as lucky as they'd like us to think!

CHARLEY What you getting at, Duncan?

DUNCAN *rises thoughtfully.*

DUNCAN Well, you look at it this way, Charley — what've the Government gained the day, eh? As far as I can see, nothing!

KATE Oh, fair's fair, Duncan! They have stopped a Revolution haven't they?

DUNCAN Aye — meantime, Kate, meantime! That's no gain as far as they're concerned! We could be planning another Revolution for next week for aa that they ken!

CHARLEY Oh, I wouldn't say that, Duncan. I mean, lots of blokes what turned out today won't be so keen to turn out again — not when they've sussed that someone's let the cat out of the bag!

DUNCAN Och, Charley, for Christ's sake use the heid, will ye? The Government dinna ken that — no for definite anyway. *(Gathers his thoughts.)* Look, I'll tell ye what *I* think — I think that the Government knew a wee bit of what was going on the day — but no enough. I dinna ken how much they *did* ken — but I suspect this much: it wasna as much as they wanted!

KATE You mean the spy — if there was a spy — didn't know enough to give them the whole story?

DUUNCAN Aye! So they played it crafty, contented themselves with keeping the barracks and Downing Street safe. *(Nods.)* They're biding their time! Now, what does that make ye think?

CHARLEY *and* KATE *don't quite take* DUNCAN'S *meaning, but before he can explain,* SOMERVILLE *enters from the right.* DUNCAN *greets him with a slight degree of suspicion.*

DUNCAN It's yersel, Sandy!
SOMERVILLE Duncan.

SOMERVILLE *and* CHARLEY *exchange nods.* KATE *rises, pleased to see* SOMERVILLE.

KATE Sandy! Where did you get to, love? We was looking all over . . .
SOMERVILLE I wasna there, Kate. I've been in the hous aa afternune.
KATE Eh?
CHARLEY We told you, Mrs B. Perhaps you'll believe us now. He got cold feet and backed out!

KATE *is momentarily speechless.*

KATE No. No. I don't believe it. You — you couldn't! Not

you, not — the Soldier! Why, you ain't afraid of anything in the whole damned world! *(Grasps at a possible explanation.)* You guessed, that's what! You sussed it out! That's right, Sandy, ain't it? You guessed what was going to happen.

SOMERVILLE *turns to* DUNCAN.

SOMERVILLE   What did happen, in any case?

DUNCAN   The haill toun was hotching with sodgers — we didna get within a hundred yards of Downing Street and ye couldna see the barracks for artillery. *(Pauses, gives* SOMERVILLE *a hard look.)* It looks unco like the work of a Government spy to me!

SOMERVILLE *nods, unperturbed.*

SOMERVILLE   Ye tell me?

Enter SALLY *from the left. She goes quickly to* KATE *and embraces her.*

SALLY   Mum! Thank God you're safe! I was so worried!

KATE   Worried? What about, girl?

SALLY   You, of course, silly! When Sandy told me what you were going to do, I thought . . .

KATE   He *told* you? Why'd you do that, Sandy? Why tell Sally?

SALLY   Because of the soldiers, of course! I was ever so worried when I saw all them soldiers — then Sandy explained to me that they were only there for your protection!

KATE   Protection!

DUNCAN   And how did you ken that, Somerville?

CHARLEY   Of course! It had to be! He was arrested on the night of . . .

SOMERVILLE *(angry)* Listen, son, when I gie my word, I keep it! *(Cooling.)* I telt Lovett and Robert Owen. The Union made a deal wi the airmy!

KATE *(almost screaming)* You bastard! ! ! What did you have to go and do that for?

87

SOMERVILLE I had to, Kate! I kent . . .

KATE, CHARLEY *and* DUNCAN *all converge on* SOMERVILLE.

KATE Get him, lads!

As the three men struggle, SALLY *tries to go to* SOMERVILLE'S *aid.*

SALLY Leave him alone! What you going to do . . .

KATE *restrains* SALLY.

KATE You stay out of this, Sally!
SALLY Leave him! Leave him be! He ain't never . . .

KATE *pulls* SALLY *away from the struggle.*

KATE Come on out of this, girl!
SALLY No! No! I won't let you!

KATE *clouts* SALLY *on the side of the head, knocking her to the floor.*

KATE I said stay out of it, girl! *(Turns to the others, who now have* SOMERVILLE *more or less under control, gripping his arms and holding him steadily as he pulls from side to side.)* Now then, lads . . . over the table with him!
SOMERVILLE Kate, dinna be sic a fool!

DUNCAN *and* CHARLEY *pull* SOMERVILLE *over the table, holding him face down on top of it.*

KATE Fool? Oh, I've been a fool all right! I'll say I've been afool! I trusted you, believed in you, I was ready at any risk and any sacrifice to stand by you! You deserted me, Sandy — you deserted and betrayed us all! Well, you dog, don't think

you'll slink off from here with your tail between your legs!
I've got just the medicine for you, my lad!

KATE *tears open* SOMERVILLE'S *shirt.* SALLY *screams and rises
to her feet.* KATE *goes to the dresser and takes out the green
bag.* SALLY *rushes to stop her.*

SALLY   No! No! Mum you can't!

KATE *brushes* SALLY *aside again.*

KATE   Leave off, girl! I'll soon show you what I can do!
(*Addresses* SOMERVILLE.) Well, Mister Hero! They let you
off the second hundred, did they? Well, we'll soon fix that
. . .

KATE *draws back the lash, but* SALLY *seizes her arm.*

SALLY   No, Mum, no! Please!

KATE *and* SALLY *struggle.*

KATE   Leave off, Sally! Leave off — or I swear I'll give you
some of this and all!

KATE *wrenches herself away from* SALLY *and turns once more
to* SOMERVILLE, *when* HARRY *bursts in from the left. Obviously
drunk, he is rather unsteady on his feet and a bottle of rum
is sticking out of his pocket.*

HARRY (*singing*)   "Oh, I am a trooper bold
                     sworn to do as I am told
                     but you shall not have my soul . . .

His voice trails away as he takes in the scene.

Here! What the fuck's all this then?
KATE   You get out of it, Harry!

89

HARRY *advances on* KATE.

HARRY   What you doing with my cat, girl? You ain't got no right . . .

KATE   Get out of it, I'm telling you!

She makes a pass at him with the lash,, but he catches hold of it and pulls it from her quite easily.

HARRY   Oh, Jesus Christ! Who told you you could use this, then? *(Takes the lash by the stock and grips it firmly.)* Skilled task, this is, you know — skilled task, no mistake! Any flogging done around here's got to be done by me! *(Snaps to attention.)* Sergeant Farrier Hampden, sir! Beg to report, sir — you show me the prisoner and I'll show you his backbone!

He swings the lash about his head. ALL *except* SOMERVILLE *dive for cover.* HARRY *and* SOMERVILLE *face each other.* SOMERVILLE *advances on* HARRY, *who still appears to be in the throes of some drunken fantasy.*

SOMERVILLE   Right, Harry. Come on.

HARRY   Here he is! Here's the prisoner! Now come along, son — you know you did wrong. Time to take your punishment!

SOMERVILLE   Come on now, Harry. Gie me the cat.

HARRY   That's what I'm here for, boy.

HARRY *raises the lash to strike* SOMERVILLE. SOMERVILLE *stands his ground and their eyes lock. The reality of the situation dawns on* HARRY *and he looks at the lash in his upraised arm as if surprised to see it there.*

HARRY   Oh, Christ!

SOMERVILLE *moves forward and takes the lash from* HARRY. *As he starts to fold it up, the others move forward, but halt*

90

abruptly as he turns to face them. HARRY, *completely oblivious to what has been going on, pulls the bottle of rum from his pocket as he staggers about.*

Sorry, Sandy! Sorry, mate. Forgot myself, didn't I? All Katie's fault — pissing about with that cat!
KATE Oh, shut up! Drunken pig!

HARRY *uncorks the bottle with his teeth, spitting away the cork. He sticks his tongue out at Kate and gives her two fingers. He takes a drink from the bottle and turns to* SOMERVILLE.

HARRY Here you are, Sandy mate! You want some of this?
SOMERVILLE No thanks, Harry.
HARRY Oh, of course! Of course! Forgot myself again, didn't I? You never touch the stuff! *(Quoting ironically.)* Take away that rum, Charley Hunter! I don't want none of it! *(Chuckles wickedly as he approaches* SOMERVILLE.*)* You want to know something, Sandy Somerville? Eh? *(Draws himself up exaggeratedly.)* Hero you may be, brave man you may be, but — my God! — what a first-class, thick-headed mug you are! I could have been shot of this lot! If you'd kept your stupid Scottish nose out of it, they could all have been half-way to Australia by this time!
CHARLEY Australia?
HARRY Yes! That surprised you, didn't it, Charley? That gave you a bit of a turn? Australia! That's where you were bound, mate! That's what Captain fucking Gillies had in mind for you!
DUNCAN Gillies? What's Captain Gillies to do with it?

HARRY *ignores* DUNCAN *and turns to* SOMERVILLE.

HARRY Not just this lot either! Not just this bunch of loonies but Lovett and Place and Owen and all the rest of them trade union trouble-makers! They'd all be on their merry way to

91

Australia if you'd done what I wanted and kept well out of it!

DUNCAN *advances on* HARRY. *All are interested and made apprehensive by what* HARRY *has said.* DUNCAN *puts his hand on* HARRY'S *arm.*

DUNCAN   Harry, what's this . . .

HARRY *brushes* DUNCAN *off.*

HARRY   Watch it, Craig! I'll fill you in, see if I don't!
KATE   Harry, what is this? What're you on about?
HARRY   No, you don't know, Katie, do you? You'd never guess! *(With hostility.)* Craig might, though — for all I know, he's in with him!
CHARLEY   What're you talking about, Harry? In with who?
HARRY   Captain Gillies, of course! So-called Captain Gillies! *(Turns to* SOMERVILLE *with a chuckle.)* Ho, ho, we can tell them a thing or two about Captain Gillies, can't we, Sandy?

Enter GILLIES.

GILLIES   What can you tell them about Captain Gillies?

His entrance surprises them. HARRY *staggers towards him.*

HARRY   I've been around long enough to know your kind when I lay eyes on him, mate!
GILLIES   Harry, you're drunk. *(Turns to* SOMERVILLE.*)* Somerville, you're still here. *(*SOMERVILLE *does not respond.)* I warned you. *(Turns to the others.)* Now, then — what's been going on here? What's been happening?
DUNCAN   We're thinking that you can maybe tell us, Captain.
GILLIES   Tell you what?
CHARLEY   Why we was betrayed today. Why all our plans came unstuck.

92

KATE Yes! And what's all this about Australia, Captain?

GILLIES Australia?

DUNCAN Aye, Harry reckons it was a put-up job from the start — and that you were at the back of it!

SALLY Only Sandy guessed what you were up to and did something about it!

GILLIES *is taken aback by this. He turns to* SOMERVILLE.

GILLIES Oh, did he now? Well, well, well — I might have known! *(Sarcastically.)* So you guessed what I was up to, eh? *(Contemptuously.)* And how the hell would *you* do that? *(Witheringly.)* Oh Somerville, I can see I was right this afternoon — I *did* over-estimate you. I thought you were a man of some intelligence, but now I can see you're just a squalid little individual like the rest! You think that just because you took a flogging — made one piffling little sacrifice! — that that was enough! *(Shakes his head.)* What does it matter if one man is flogged? What does it matter if six illiterate peasants are shipped off to the colonies? How far does that take us down the Revolutionary road? It gives your friends, Lovett and Owen, something to gossip about, that's all — provides the populace with a few heroes to drool over! I suppose you thought you were being noble today? Preventing bloodshed or some such nonsense? Well, let me tell you, Somerville, bloodshed is exactly what the people need! Blood, blood and more blood! The people will never take a single step against the tyrants until they see the blood of their friends and their relatives and their work-mates gushing down the gutters of this land!

KATE *(in alarm)* Harry was right! It was an ambush! It was you who was leading us into it, you who betrayed us!

GILLIES Betrayed you? Of course I betrayed you! What do you matter? What does any single one of us matter? In the People's Cause, I'd betray my own mother — I'd betray myself! The true Revolutionary can never afford to take account of the distinctions of the individual! We have to

93

know that it's never enough to fight once — we have to fight and fight and fight again! We have to know that we will only come near to victory if we dedicate all our ambitions, hopes, loves, fears, our entire future to the People's Cause! We have to know even that if we die in the struggle, there will be no praise for us, no glory — we'll bite the dust just like anyone else! We have no room for such vanities as praise or glory or individualistic ambition. All ambition has to serve the Revolution — all praise and glory must go to the collective struggle! *(Turns with menace to* SOMERVILLE.*)* We have no heroes — or traitors or knaves. One man's courage, cowardice, treachery is of no consequence — unless the Revolution is served by it. *(Takes a step towards* SOMERVILLE.*)* You can be a hero in the bourgeois world, Somerville, but not in ours!

SOMERVILLE *lets out the lash.* ALL, *including* GILLIES, *step back with a gasp. Slowly,* SOMERVILLE *moves towards* GILLIES, *deliberately folding the tails of the lash as he does so. He halts a pace in front of* GILLIES, *takes a deep breath, then holds out the folded lash. He drops it at* GILLIE'S *feet. Exit* SOMER- VILLE *to the right. As* GILLIES *stoops to pick up the lash, the others exchange nods and glances and exit to the left.*

GILLIES   Kate! Duncan! Charley! Where are you . . . come back, damn you! I did it for all of us, don't you see? All of us . . .

He checks his step, turns and looks to the right, then to the lash in his hand. He lets out the tails, gives out a furious bellow — and whips the lash across the table.

GILLIES *(to himself)* We have no room for heroes — and we never will.